YOUR COLLEGE EXPERIENCE

Strategies for Success

Concise Eighth Edition

John N. Gardner

Distinguished Professor Emeritus, Library and Information Science
Senior Fellow, National Resource Center for the First-Year Experience
and Students in Transition
University of South Carolina–Columbia

Executive Director, Policy Center on the First Year of College
Brevard, North Carolina

A. Jerome Jewler

Distinguished Professor Emeritus, School of Journalism
and Mass Communications, College of Mass Communications
and Information Studies
University of South Carolina–Columbia

Betsy O. Barefoot

Codirector and Senior Scholar
Policy Center on the First Year of College
Brevard, North Carolina

BEDFORD/ST. MARTIN'S

Boston ◆ New York

For Bedford/St. Martin's

Executive Editor: Carrie Brandon
Developmental Editor: Julie Kelly
Production Editor: Kerri A. Cardone
Senior Production Supervisor: Dennis J. Conroy
Marketing Manager: Casey Carroll
Editorial Assistants: Sarah Guariglia and Nicholas Murphy
Copyeditor: Ellen Kaplan-Maxfield
Text Design: Diane Beaseley
Cover Design: Donna Lee Dennison
Composition: Pre-Press PMG
Printing and Binding: R R Donnelley & Sons

President: Joan E. Feinberg
Editorial Director: Denise B. Wydra
Director of Marketing: Karen R. Soeltz
Director of Editing, Design, and Production: Marcia Cohen
Assistant Director of Editing, Design, and Production: Elise S. Kaiser
Managing Editor: Elizabeth M. Schaaf

Library of Congress Control Number: 2008935057

Manufactured in the United States of America.

3 2 1 0 9
f e d c b

For information, write: Bedford/St. Martin's, 75 Arlington Street, Boston, MA 02116   (617-399-4000)

ISBN-10: 0-312-68302-2 (Student Edition)
ISBN-13: 978-0-312-68302-3

ISBN-10: 0-312-68303-0 (Annotated Instructor's Edition)
ISBN-13: 978-0-312-68303-0

About the Authors

John N. Gardner brings unparalleled experience to this authoritative text for first-year seminar courses. John is the recipient of his institution's highest award for teaching excellence. He has twenty-five years of experience directing and teaching in the most respected and widely emulated first-year seminar in the country, the *University 101* course at the University of South Carolina. John is universally recognized as one of the country's leading educators for his role in initiating and orchestrating an international reform movement to improve the beginning college experience, a concept he coined as *the first-year experience.* He is the founding executive director of two influential higher education centers that support campuses in their efforts to improve the learning and retention of beginning college students: the National Resource Center for the First-Year Experience and Students in Transition at the University of South Carolina (www.sc.edu/fye), and the Policy Center on the First Year of College in Brevard, NC (www.firstyear.org). The experiential basis for all of his work is his own miserable first year of college spent on academic probation, an experience he hopes to prevent for this book's readers. Today, as a much happier adult, John is married to a fellow author of this book, Betsy Barefoot.

A. Jerome Jewler is a best-selling author, educator, and friend to students. As distinguished professor emeritus of the College of Mass Communications and Information Studies as well as codirector of the *University 101* first-year seminar—including its faculty development component—at the University of South Carolina–Columbia, he has guided advertising students through the creative and writing processes, taught doctoral candidates how to teach mass communication courses, and helped hundreds of new students determine their goals. As *University 101* codirector, he has planned and conducted training workshops for first-year seminar instructors, won a Mortar Board award for teaching excellence, and was recognized as USC Advisor of the Year as well as nationally acclaimed as the Distinguished Advertising Educator in 2000. Currently, he is teaching younger children subjects from Napoleon to dinosaurs to art as a volunteer docent for the South Carolina State Museum.

Betsy O. Barefoot is a writer, researcher, and teacher whose special area of scholarship is the first year of college. During her tenure at the University of South Carolina from 1988 to 1999, she served as codirector for research and publications at the National Resource Center for the First-Year Experience and Students in Transition. She taught *University 101,* in addition to special topic graduate courses on the first-year experience and the principles of college teaching. She conducts first-year seminar faculty training workshops around the U.S. and in other countries and is frequently called on to evaluate first-year seminar outcomes. Betsy currently serves as codirector and senior scholar in the Policy Center on the First Year of College in Brevard, NC. In this role she led a major national research project to identify institutions of excellence on the first year of college. She currently works with both two- and four-year campuses in evaluating all components of the first year.

Brief Contents

Contents

Preface for Students

Question

How many American colleges and universities offer a first-year seminar or college success course?

a) I think my campus is the only one.

b) Maybe about half—I really don't know.

c) I've heard that almost all colleges and universities offer a special course to help students like me be successful.

If you picked answer **C**, you're right. Recent research conducted by the Policy Center on the First Year of College found that over 90 percent of higher education institutions in the U.S. offer such a course.

First-year seminars/college success courses are different from other courses you will take in your first year. And this book is different from all of your other textbooks. In fact, it may be the most important book you read as you begin your college experience because it's about you and improving your chances for success in college and beyond.

The very fact that you are even reading this book means your campus offers a course designed to help first-year college students. One thing we know is that if you successfully complete this course, your chances of continuing in college and completing your degree are greater than those of students who do not take advantage of this opportunity.

We know that college can be very difficult and that you will face many challenges ahead. But we also know that many experiences you have in college will be really enjoyable. This book will help you take advantage of all that college has to offer.

Why listen to us? For one thing, all three of us have dedicated our higher education careers to helping improve what educators have come to call *the first-year experience*. Many professionals in our field would probably agree that we are three of the country's leading experts on promoting college success in college as well as champions for all new college students. All three of us met and became friends and coworkers at the University of South Carolina. All three of us taught USC's internationally known *University 101* first-year seminar, where we developed and practiced many of the strategies we provide in this book. In our current work, we help colleges and universities around the U.S. investigate and improve the way they design experiences in the first year, both in and out of the classroom.

You probably have some questions you would like answered before you even start reading this book. Here are some of the most common questions we hear from students across the country.

Why should I take this course?

Research conducted by colleges and universities all over the world has found that first-year students are far more likely to be successful and to graduate if they participate in courses, programs, and activities designed to teach them *how to do college*. That is the basic purpose of this course. It isn't a course for dummies but rather is intentionally designed to help you avoid some of the pitfalls that trip up many beginning students.

Aren't all the topics covered in this book common sense? I know how to read and study, and I have lots of experience with relationships and wellness.

Although you have probably been exposed to some of the information you'll learn in this course, college is a totally different environment. Topics such as relationships and personal health become even more important when you're living away from home in an apartment or campus residence hall. Even if you're living with your family, college will challenge you to manage your time, feel comfortable interacting with professors, and study effectively. Mastering these skills will be a focus of this course.

What am I going to get out of this course?

Most important, this course offers a supportive environment in which you will be able to share your successes and your frustrations, get to know others who are also beginning college, and develop a lasting relationship with your instructor. In the process you will feel more knowledgeable about and secure in your present environment. You will also be encouraged to think about the future and begin making plans for life after college, whether that involves a job or in pursuing additional education in graduate or professional school.

Doing everything this book suggests might seem easy while you are reading about it, but putting this information into practice is a different matter—and that's what we are going to show you how to do. Generally speaking, if you can apply the ideas in this book to your everyday life, you will be more likely to graduate and to achieve your life goals. Welcome to college!

John N. Gardner
A. Jerome Jewler
Betsy O. Barefoot

Preface for Instructors

Anyone who teaches beginning college students knows how they are changing from year to year. Today's students are increasingly job-focused, technologically adept, and unevenly prepared for the academic requirements of college. Engaging and retaining students is a challenge at all levels but particularly so in the first year.

Since the early 1980s, college and university educators have recognized the first-year seminar as a powerful tool in an overall plan to improve college success. But as students themselves change, so do these courses. Helping students develop a clear sense of purpose in college, assisting them in making the right choice of academic major, and engaging them in learning, especially through the use of technology, are goals of today's seminar courses.

In order to make *Your College Experience* usable in more classrooms and in more situations, we have created this less-expensive, more streamlined *Concise Edition,* which contains the most commonly taught chapters from the bigger book—those chapters that reviewers told us were most relevant to all kinds of students at all kinds of schools. This new edition responds to the changing needs of first-year students. It continues discussion of timeless issues—learning strategies, critical thinking, time management, relationships, personal health, and so forth. But it adds a new focus on purpose and life planning. Most chapters include a new feature, *Wired Window,* to develop students' awareness of the implications of technology.

Although this eighth edition of *Your College Experience: Strategies for Success,* Concise Edition has been significantly revised, it continues to be based on our collective knowledge and experience in teaching first-year students as well as on feedback from generations of student users. Because it is also grounded in a growing body of research on college success and retention, we are confident that if students read and heed the information herein, they are more likely to become engaged in the college experience, to learn more, and to persist to graduation.

This book is designed for students in both two- and four-year residential and commuter institutions. Our intent always has been to write in a way that conveys respect and admiration for students by treating them as the adults we know they are, all the while recognizing their continuing need for challenge and support.

Whether you are considering this textbook for use in your first-year seminar or already have made a decision to adopt it, we thank you for your interest and trust that you will find this textbook a valuable teaching aid. Although our text was written primarily for students in first-year seminar courses, we hope it will also guide you and your institution in understanding the range of issues that, for better or for worse, affect college success in each year of college. Whether you are a first-time adopter of this text or someone who has used previous editions, we want you to know the essential features of this text and the major differences between this edition and the previous ones.

An Organization Based on Enduring, Time-Tested Coverage

The first two chapters of the book set the stage by outlining fundamental strategies—applicable to students of any age at any type of institution—for college success. A new Chapter 1, "Exploring Your Purpose in Attending College," encourages students to think about their purpose in attending college and to apply that purpose to both short- and long-term goal-setting. Chapter 2, "Time and Money Management," includes advice for improving students' understanding of these finite fundamental resources. Chapters 3 through 9 introduce students to the essential skills for academic success—how to listen, take notes, remember lecture and text material, and take tests. Other chapters cover the important topics of critical thinking and engagement with learning—of becoming an active participant in the learning process. Chapters 10 through 12 help students better understand themselves now and in the future. Chapter 10 focuses on values, particularly on how new students can explore their values in service learning. Chapter 11 on diversity is designed to help new students take maximum advantage of the diversity they will encounter in their college or university. Diversity is not only a part of college life but also a defining characteristic of our world. The final chapter is a candid exploration of issues related to physical and mental health that addresses how students can care for their bodies and minds in college and beyond.

New to the Eighth Edition

Coverage has been revised in large and small ways to reflect a new focus on purpose and life planning as well as on key academic topics. Here are what we consider to be key themes of *Your College Experience: Strategies for Success,* Concise Eighth Edition, along with selected examples of new coverage.

Purposes in attending college and goals for getting the most out of the experience providing context for the course and for the book, the new opening chapter, "Exploring Your Purpose in Attending College," asks students to consider the importance of college education both to society and to their own personal goals. Students are encouraged to view college as an opportunity to learn to think more critically and to act more responsibly, markedly changing their lives for the better.

Revised and expanded material addresses new and growing issues in students' worlds including managing time and money, avoiding academic dishonesty, achieving academic literacy, and welcoming diversity on campus. Chapter 2, "Time and Money Management," presents a revised section on respecting others' time and being mindful of the ways others choose to use their time. It also includes expanded tips for wise usage of popular credit and debit cards. Chapter 8, "Reading and Remembering," offers advice on making the most of college reading, including a discussion of how it differs from other reading. Chapter 9, "Doing Your Best on Exams and Tests," offers expanded coverage of academic dishonesty, including straightforward discussion of cheating and plagiarism as well as a new section on how to study for exams. Chapter 11, "Diversity: Appreciating Differences Among Us," broadens this important topic to discuss diversity in terms of age, learning and physical ability, gender, and sexual orientation.

A focus on "learning for a lifetime" helps students see that the decisions they make today can help them later in life. This focus also helps students aim to be lifelong learners, not just learners in a college setting. Chapter 4, "Majors and Careers: Making the Right Choice," has a new section entitled "Getting Off to a Good Start in the Workplace" that identifies behaviors employers are looking for in new employees versus ones that can be grounds for termination. Chapter 5, "Engagement with Learning," includes a new section on the importance of collaboration in the workplace.

Chapter Features

Revised and expanded features in each chapter provide even more support for actively engaging students and turning them into self-directed learners.

▶ *Chapter Opening Quizzes* on upcoming chapter content—modeled on popular magazine quizzes—engage students by giving them a peek at what a chapter is about. Assessing their responses, students can quickly see what they know and what they stand to gain from reading each chapter.

▶ NEW *Wired Window* boxes provide practical advice on how to make use of technology in light of each chapter topic. Although today's students are tech-savvy, they might not have considered how technology is implemented in college.

▶ NEW *Confessions of a College Student* boxes introduce readers to real students who have mastered chapter topics and illustrate how practical skills detailed in each chapter apply to readers' own lives.

▶ **Revised prompts for writing and discussion** get students engaged and connected. These boxes throughout the text provide opportunities to discuss, write, blog, and journal about issues covered in the book, allowing students to explore how key topics relate to them personally. The questions also help instructors gear course work to students' needs.

▶ **Revised *Where to Go for Help* boxes** provide handy reference lists of valid sources of information and assistance. Students often don't know where to get help when they need it. This important feature directs students to helpful resources both on campus and online and gives them a place to write notes on resources specific to their campus.

▶ **Unique *Building Your Portfolio* assignments** help students assemble a collection of their own work. Because portfolios are a useful tool not only for assessment but also for self-realization, a new assignment at the end of each chapter gives students step-by-step help in creating a collection that can be continued long after they finish the course.

Supplements

Instructor Resources

▶ **Annotated Instructor's Edition** This instructor's edition supplements the full text of the student edition with annotations and suggestions for teaching, updated and revised by Heidi Jung of Southern Illinois University–Carbondale (SIUC). As an Instructional Designer at SIUC, Heidi has been providing instructional support to faculty for over twelve years, identifying strategies to improve teaching and learning. This experience makes her an excellent guide for adopters of *Your College Experience: Strategies for Success,* Concise Eighth Edition.

▶ **Instructor's Manual and Test Bank** Revised by Heidi Jung of Southern Illinois University–Carbondale, the Instructor's Manual and Test Bank includes chapter objectives, teaching suggestions, additional exercises, test questions, a list of common concerns of first-year students, an introduction to the first-year experience course, a sample lesson plan for each chapter, and various case studies relevant to topics covered. Heidi teaches the New Student Seminar course on the SIUC campus using *Your College Experience* and has revised this edition of the Instructor's Manual to include plentiful ideas on how to effectively teach using the book. For the new edition she has also written new test bank questions for every chapter to update these for today's students (ISBN-10: 0-312-68304-9; ISBN-13: 978-0-312-68304-7).

▶ **VideoCentral** is a growing collection of videos for the college success classroom. Meet academic, real world, and student writers and listen to tips on writing for the classroom and for life. Hear from real students discussing their own experiences transitioning to college life. Available in Fall 2009.

See your local Bedford/St. Martin's sales representative for more information.

Student Resources

▶ *Your College Experience* **Student Central** website (bedfordstmartins.com/collegeexpconcise) offers a variety of rich learning resources designed to enhance the student experience. These resources include video tips from real students, self-awareness exercises to assess your students' strengths and weaknesses, quick guides to refresh basic skills in grammar, writing, and reading, downloadable podcasts for quick study tips, and more.

▶ *The Bedford/St. Martin's Planner with Grammar Girl's Quick and Dirty Tips* Includes everything that students need to plan and use their time effectively, offering advice on preparing schedules and to-do lists and providing blank schedules and calendars (monthly and weekly) for planning. Integrated into the planner are tips from the popular *Grammar Girl* podcast (and from other podcast hosts); quick advice on fixing common grammar errors, note-taking, and succeeding on tests; an address book; and an annotated list of useful websites. The planner fits easily into a backpack or purse so students can take it anywhere (ISBN-10: 0-312-48023-7; ISBN-13: 978-0-312-48023-3).

Acknowledgments

Special thanks to the reviewers of this edition whose wisdom and suggestions guided its creation: Rachel A. Beech, Arizona State University–Polytechnic; Paula Bradberry, Arkansas State University; Stella Fox, Nassau Community College; Khalida I. Haqq, Mercer County Community College; Elizabeth Hicks, Central Connecticut State University; Darby Johnsen, Oklahoma City Community College; and Debra Olsen, Madison Area Technical College.

We would like to thank the numerous colleagues who have contributed to this book in its previous editions as well as in this edition. They are Michelle Murphy Burcin, University of South Carolina–Columbia; James B. Craig, University of California–Irvine; Juan Flores, Folsom Lake College; Philip Gardner, Michigan State University; Jeanne L. Higbee, University of Minnesota–Twin Cities; John M. Whiteley, University of California–Irvine; and Edward Zlotkowski, Bentley College.

Finally, life is full of unexpected changes even in the world of college-text publishing. When we started our work on this edition, it was to have been published by Cengage Learning. However, during the production period, an outstanding college-text publisher, Bedford/St. Martin's, acquired our titles. We respect and appreciate the contributions of our former Cengage team in helping us to reach and assist hundreds of thousands of new college students. As we look to the future, we are excited about the contributions the Bedford/St. Martin's team will make to improve our work. Our special thanks to our team at Cengage Learning: Annie Todd, Director of College Success, Cengage Learning; Laurie Runion, Development Editor; Reynol Junco, *Wired Window* feature; Maggie Barbieri, Editor of *Confessions of a College Student*.

At Bedford/St. Martin's, we thank Joan Feinberg, President; Denise Wydra, Editorial Director; Karen Henry, Editor in Chief; Carrie Brandon, Executive Editor; Julie Kelly, Development Editor; Casey Carroll, Marketing Manager; Sarah Guariglia, Editorial Assistant; Nicholas Murphy, Editorial Assistant; Elise Kaiser, Assistant Director of Editing, Design, and Production; and Kerri Cardone, Production Editor.

Most of all, we thank you, the readers of our book, for you are the true inspiration for this work.

Exploring Your Purpose for Attending College

In this chapter YOU WILL LEARN

▶ What college is all about

▶ The many purposes of college

▶ The importance of thinking about your own purpose for college

▶ How college "levels the playing field" for students from different backgrounds

▶ The many differences between high school and college

▶ The challenges of being an adult or returning student

▶ The benefits of a college education

© John Boykin/PhotoEdit

What Is Your PURPOSE FOR ATTENDING College?

Read the following questions and choose the answer that most fits you.

1 What is the reason you decided to come to college?

(A) I have a lot of reasons—some are related to what I plan to do when I graduate, but I also just want to learn about different things and have lots of different experiences.

(B) I think that if you want a good job, you have to go to college. That's the real reason I'm here.

(C) I really don't know why I'm here. All of my other friends were applying to colleges, so I thought I should. It seemed like a good idea when I applied—it's better than working or joining the military.

2 Why do you think there are so many colleges and universities in the United States?

(A) I think the U.S. and most other countries really value education and believe it's important for everyone.

(B) I didn't know there were many colleges and universities. I only know of about ten of them.

(C) I'm not sure. Maybe it has something to do with needing a lot of football teams.

3 Do you think college will help you change in positive ways?

(A) I'm looking forward to learning, meeting people, and having new experiences. I know I'll change for the better.

(B) I'm not sure whether I'll change for the better or for the worse. My family is concerned that I won't be the same person.

(C) Change? What do you mean? I think I'm OK just as I am, and I don't think I need to change anything I think or believe.

4 Do you understand the importance of critical thinking?

(A) There are so many false claims everywhere you look; it's really important to learn how to analyze evidence by thinking critically and to arrive at logical conclusions.

(B) Well, some things can be debated, but others are absolutely the truth. I don't need to think critically about everything.

(C) I'm not sure I even know what critical thinking is. Does it mean being critical of others?

5 What do you think it means to be a responsible college student?

(A) I think being responsible means managing my new freedom, keeping up with my work, and making the most of all my opportunities.

(B) I know what my parents would say: It's important for me to be a good student. But I also think it's my responsibility to take advantage of all the new social opportunities.

(C) Not flunking out.

Review your responses. (A) responses indicate that you have a good beginning understanding of what's important in college, but you'll still need to work on maintaining those skills. (B) responses indicate that you're a good student who is thinking about the purpose of college, but there's always room for improvement. (C) responses indicate that you need some help in understanding college and why you're here. This course and this book can help you develop the understanding and motivation you need to be a successful college student.

In 1900 fewer than 2 percent of Americans of traditional college age attended college. Today, new technologies and the information explosion are changing the workplace so drastically that few people can support themselves and their families adequately without some education beyond high school. College is so important that more than 60 percent of high school graduates (more than 17 million students) attend. Because higher education can be essential to your future earning power and your overall well-being, we are committed to providing a set of strategies for you to do your best. That's what this book is all about.

As you're settling into your new college routine, we would like to welcome you to the world of higher education. The fact that you are reading this textbook probably means that you are enrolled in a first-year seminar or "college success" course designed to introduce you to college and help you make the most of it. In this chapter,

◀ **Each of these students probably defines the purpose of college differently.**

we'll discuss how you fit into the whole idea of college. We'll consider why the U.S. has more colleges and universities than any other country in the world. We'll also help you explore the purposes of college—many that your college might define for you. But even more important, we'll help you define your purposes for being here.

The College Experience

So what is the college experience? Depending on who you are, your life circumstances, and why you decided to enroll, college can mean different things. College is often portrayed in books and film as a place where young people live away from home in ivy-covered residence halls and "find" themselves. Many students do find out a lot about themselves, and we hope you will, too. But today most students don't move away from home, don't live on campus, and don't see much ivy. We often see college portrayed as a place with a major focus on big-time sports, heavy drinking, and partying. And, yes, there is some of that at some colleges. But college is really far more than any single image you might carry around in your head.

Write • DISCUSS • Compare • Ask • BLOG • Answer • *Journal*

> So far, is life at your college or university what you expected or hoped for? Why or why not?

There are many ways to define college. For starters, college is an established process designed by society to further formal education, so that students who attend and graduate will be prepared for roles in what has become known as "the information economy." Basically, that means that most college graduates are going to be earning their living by creating, managing, and using information. Because the amount of available information expands all the time, your college classes can't possibly teach you all you need to know for years to come. The most important skill you'll need to learn in college is how to keep learning throughout your life.

Why College Is Important to Our Society

American society obviously values higher education, which explains why the U.S. has so many colleges and universities—more than 4,100. College is the primary way that people achieve "upward social mobility," or the ability to attain a higher standard of living. In earlier centuries, a high standard of living was almost always a function of family background. You were either born into power and money or you spent your life working for others who had power and money. But in most countries today, receiving a college degree helps "level the playing field" for everyone. A college degree equalizes differences due to background, race, ethnicity, national origin, immigration status, family lineage, and personal connections. Simply put, college participation is about ensuring that more people have the opportunity to be evaluated on the basis of merit rather than by family status, money, or other forms of privilege. It makes achieving the "American dream" possible.

Write • DISCUSS • Compare • Ask • BLOG • Answer • *Journal*

> When you hear the phrase "American dream," what do you think of?
> How would you describe the meaning of these words to someone else?

College is also important because it is society's primary means of preparing citizens for leadership roles. Without a college degree, it is much more difficult to be a leader in a community, company, profession, or the military.

A four-year college degree also prepares students for continuing their education in a graduate or professional school. If you want to become a medical doctor, dentist, lawyer, or college professor, four years of college is just the beginning.

Why College Is Important for You

College is about thinking and will help you understand how to become a "critical thinker"—someone who doesn't believe everything he or she hears or reads but instead looks for evidence before forming an opinion. Developing critical-thinking skills will empower you to make sound decisions throughout your life.

Although college is often thought of as a time when traditional-age students become young adults, we realize that many of you are already adults. Whatever your age, college can also be a time when you take some risks, learn new things, and meet new and different people—all in a relatively safe environment. It's OK to experiment in college, within limits, because that's what college is designed for.

WIRED WINDOW

THE INTERNET OFFERS a number of ways to get connected online. As you might know, social networking websites like Facebook and MySpace are a great way to connect to your friends. Is Facebook popular at your college? If so, take advantage of its networking potential. Through Facebook you can find new schoolmates with similar interests, join clubs or interest groups, and find friends in your classes. Keep in mind that the information you post on Facebook is available to everyone in your network unless you adjust your privacy settings. While most students use Facebook and MySpace appropriately, some students have faced institutional (and sometimes legal) sanctions for pictures and information they posted online. Therefore, it is important that you review your profile to make sure you are including only information that you want the public to know about you.

Another way you can learn about your specific college is by taking advantage of official and unofficial online campus resources. Your institution's website is one official resource that is useful for finding a range of information, from how to get help with your writing to when the term break begins. Unofficial resources include websites that rate professors and student-run wikis to help you find answers to common questions about your college or university. A popular website for rating professors is http://www.RateMyProfessor.com. Keep in mind that ratings on these websites are not reviewed for accuracy, so use them only as a starting point to learn about a professor.

College will provide you many opportunities for developing a variety of *social* networks. You will find both formal and informal networking opportunities that will help you make friends and develop alliances with faculty and fellow students who share your interests and goals.

College, for many students, is also a good time. College definitely can be fun, and we hope it will be for you. You will meet new people, go to athletic events and parties, build camaraderie with new friends, and feel a sense of school spirit. Many college graduates relive memories of college days throughout their lives, fanatically root for their institution's athletic teams, return to homecoming year after year, and encourage their own children to attend their alma mater. In fact, you might be a "legacy"—someone whose parents or grandparents attended the same institution.

In addition to being fun, college is also a lot of work. Being a college student means hours studying each week, late nights, high-stakes exams, and working harder than you thought you could. For many students, college becomes much like a job, with defined duties, expectations, and obligations.

But most important, college will be a set of experiences designed to help you further define and achieve your own purpose. Right now, you might feel that you know exactly what you want to do with your life—where you want to go from here. Or, if you're like many students, you might be struggling to find where you fit in life and work. It is possible that as you discover more about yourself and your abilities, your purpose for coming to college will change. In fact, the vast majority of college students will change their academic major at least once during the college years, and some students will find they need to transfer to another institution in order to meet their academic goals.

But first, how would you describe your reasons for being in college and at this particular college? Perhaps you, like the vast majority of college students, see college as the pathway to a good job. Maybe you are in college to train or retrain for an occupation or you have recently experienced an upheaval in your life. Perhaps you are here to fulfill a lifelong dream of getting an education. Or maybe you are bored or in a rut and looking for more pizzazz in your life. College should provide some of that. Many students enter college without a purpose that is clearly thought out. They have just been swept along by life's events and, now, here they are.

Write • DISCUSS • Compare • Ask • BLOG • Answer • *Journal*

How would you describe your reasons for coming to college at this time in your life? Do you think your reasons will change during your college career? Why or why not?

Your college or university might require you to select a major during or prior to the first year, even before you've figured out your own purpose for college. Some institutions will allow you to be "undecided" or "no preference" for a year or two. Even if you're ready to select a major, it's a good idea to keep an open mind. There are so many avenues to pursue while you're in college—many that you might not have even considered. Or, you might learn that the career you always dreamed of isn't what you thought at all. You'll learn more about choosing a major and a career later in this book, but you ought to use your first year to explore and think about your purpose for college and how that might connect with the rest of your life.

Outcomes of College

Not only can a college degree clearly make you more professionally marketable, but the college experience can enrich your life in many other ways. We hope you will take advantage of the many opportunities you'll have to learn the skills of leadership, experience diversity, explore other countries and cultures, clarify your beliefs and values, and make decisions about the rest of your life—not just what you want to do but, more important, how you want to live.

Many college graduates report that higher education changed them for the better. Based on their college experiences, you can anticipate the following:

▶ You will learn how to accumulate knowledge.

▶ You will be more likely to seek appropriate information before making a decision. Such information will also help you realize how our lives are shaped by global and local, political, social, psychological, economic, environmental, and physical forces.

▶ You will grow intellectually through interactions with cultures, languages, ethnic groups, religions, nationalities, and socioeconomic groups other than your own.

▶ You will gain self-esteem and self-confidence, which will help you realize how you might make a difference in the world.

▶ You will tend to be more flexible in your views, more future-oriented, more willing to appreciate differences of opinion, and more interested in political and public affairs.

▶ You will have children who are more likely to have greater learning potential, which in turn will help them to achieve more in life.

▶ You will be an efficient consumer, save more money, make better investments, and spend more money on home, intellectual and cultural interests, as well as on your children.

▶ You will be able to deal with bureaucracies, the legal system, tax laws, and advertising claims.

▶ You will spend more time and money on education, hobbies, and civic and community affairs.

▶ Finally, you will be more concerned with wellness and preventive health care, and, through diet, exercise, stress management, a positive attitude, and other factors, live longer and suffer fewer disabilities.

When you made the decision to come to college, you probably didn't think about all of the positive ways that college could affect the rest of your life. Your reasons for coming might have been more personal and more immediate. There are all sorts of reasons, circumstances, events, and pressures that bring students to college, and when you put different people with different motivations and purposes together, it creates an interesting environment for learning.

How College Graduates Are Different

We know without a doubt that college makes your life different from the one you would have had if you had never been a college student. Consider the list below. You'll note that the first item on the list is that college graduates earn more money. (Look at Table 1.1 to see exactly how much more.) However, note that these differences go far beyond making more money. When compared to noncollege graduates, those who graduate from college are more likely to:

▶ earn more money
▶ have a less erratic job history
▶ earn more promotions
▶ have fewer children
▶ be more involved in their children's school lives
▶ have more discretionary time and money to raise their children
▶ become leaders in their communities and employment settings
▶ stay married longer to the same person
▶ be elected to public office
▶ participate in and enjoy the arts

Table 1.1 **Median* Earnings by Educational Attainment for Year-Round, Full-Time Workers Age 25+**

Advanced degree	$63,076
Bachelor's degree	$50,960
Associate degree	$36,764
High school graduate	$31,148
Less than high school diploma	$22,568

* These are median earnings, meaning half the group earned less and half the group earned more. These figures are annualized based on weekly data through the second quarter of 2007.

Source: U.S. Department of Labor, Bureau of Labor Statistics, 2007. (http://data.bls.gov/cgi-bin/surveymost)

When compared to nongraduates, college graduates are less likely to:

▶ be imprisoned

▶ become dependent on alcohol or drugs

▶ be duped, conned, or swindled

▶ be involuntarily unemployed

▶ use tobacco products

These outcomes dramatically increase the value of your investment in college.

How College Differs from High School

As you think about your new life in college, it will help you to be clear from the outset on some of the ways that college is unique. If you just graduated from high school, you'll find some distinct differences. For instance, you will probably be part of a more diverse student body, not just in terms of race but also in terms of age, religion, political opinions, and life experiences. If you attend a large college or university, you might feel like a number—not as special as you felt in high school. You will have more potential friends to choose from, but your old ways of categorizing potential friends might not work for you. Familiar assumptions about people based on where they live, where they go to church, or what high school they attend might no longer apply to the new people you're meeting.

Although you will be able to choose from many more types of courses compared to high school, managing your time is sure to be more complex. Your classes will meet on various days and at different times, and you will have additional commitments such as work, family, activities, and sports. You might live away from home, which means that no one will check to make sure you're out of bed and on your way to class.

Compared to high school, your college classes might have many more students in them and meet for longer time periods. College tests are given less frequently—sometimes only twice a term—and you will probably be required to do more writing in college. You will be encouraged to do original research and to investigate

© image 100/Alamy

◄ **Managing your time in college can be a major challenge.**

differing points of view on a topic. You will be expected to study outside class, to prepare assignments, do assigned reading, and be ready for in-class discussions. Your instructors might rely far less on textbooks and far more on lectures than did your high school teachers. They will rarely monitor your progress; you're on your own. But you will have more freedom to express views that are different from your instructors. They will usually have their own offices and keep regular office hours.

Write • DISCUSS • Compare • Ask • BL□G • Answer • *Journal*

In what ways are you already finding that college is different from high school? Did you anticipate these differences? Why or why not?

Challenges and Opportunities for Adult and Returning Students

If you're a returning student, someone who has experienced college already, or if you are an adult living and working off-campus, you also might find that college presents new challenges and opportunities. For instance, college might feel liberating, like a new beginning, a stimulating challenge, or a path to a career. However, working full-time and attending college at night and on weekends can add stress, especially with a family at home.

You will tend to work harder than younger students because you realize how important an education can be. Consequently, you will probably earn higher grades even though you might believe you won't be able to keep up with your younger classmates. Your age and life experience will give you a unique and rich perspective on what you're learning, a perspective that most eighteen-year-olds lack.

First-Year Motivation and Commitment

What attitudes and behaviors will help you achieve your goals and be successful in college? If you are fresh out of high school, it will be important for you to learn to deal with newfound freedom. Your college professors are not going to tell you what, how, or when to study. If you live on campus, your parents won't be able to wake you in the morning, see that you eat properly and get enough sleep, monitor whether or how well you do your homework, or remind you to allow enough time to get to class. In almost every aspect of your life, you will have to assume primary responsibility for your own attitudes and behaviors.

If you are an adult student, the opposite is also true: You might experience a daunting lack of freedom. Working, caring for a family, and meeting other adult commitments and responsibilities will compete for the time and attention it takes to do your best or even simply to stay in college.

Whatever challenges you are facing, what will motivate you to be successful? And what about the enormous investment of time and money that getting a college degree requires? Are you convinced that the investment will pay off? The following list might include some of your thoughts:

▶ This is the first time someone has not been there to tell me I had to do something. Will I be able to handle all this freedom? Or will I just waste time?

▶ I've never been away from home before, and I don't know anybody. How am I going to make friends? How can I get involved in some activities? Whom do I go to for help when I need it?

▶ I have responsibilities at home. Can I get through college and still manage to take care of my family? What will my family think of all the time I'll have to spend in classes and studying?

▶ As a minority student, will I be in for any unpleasant experiences?

▶ Maybe college will be too difficult for me. I hear college teachers are much more demanding than high school teachers.

▶ I hope I won't disappoint the people I care about who expect so much of me.

▶ In high school, I got by without working too hard. Now I'll really have to study. Will I be tempted to cut corners or maybe even cheat?

▶ Will I like my roommate? What if he or she is really different from me?

▶ How will I know whether I've picked the right major? What if I don't know which major is right for me?

▶ Can I afford college? Can my parents afford it? I wouldn't want them to spend this much and then have me fail.

▶ Maybe I'm the only one who's feeling like this. Maybe everyone else is just smarter than I am.

▶ Looking around class makes me feel so old! Will I be able to keep up at my age?

Thoughts like these are very common. Although your classmates might not say it out loud, many of them share your concerns, doubts, and fears. This course will be a safe place for you to talk about all of these issues with people who care about you and your success in college.

Write • DISCUSS • Compare • Ask • BLOG • Answer • *Journal*

> On a scale of 1 to 5 with 5 being high, rate your own level of motivation for college. What do you think accounts for your current motivation level? If you don't think you are motivated, what strategies can you think of that would help motivate you?

What's Your Purpose in College?

Consider these differences in the way a student might feel about college:

I belong in college. . . . . vs. . . . . .What am I doing here?

Where would you fall between these opposite attitudes? You might find that your exact position shifts, depending on what's going on in your academic and personal life. But no matter how you feel on any given day, as you begin college you will need to spend time sorting out your own sense of purpose and level of motivation. The clearer you are about why you're in college, the easier it will be to stay motivated, even when times are tough.

To build a clearer sense of purpose, look around you and get to know other students who work hard to be successful. Identify students who have the same major or the same career interests and learn about the courses they have taken, work experiences they have had, and their plans for the future. Look for courses that are relevant to your interests, but don't stop there. Seek relevance in those required general education courses that might seem to be a waste of time or energy at first. Remember

Confessions of a College Student

Name: Valeria Maya Fernandez

Age: 18

University: University of Texas at El Paso (UTEP)

Hometown: El Paso, Texas

Major: Business: Computer Information Systems

Favorite book(s): *The Alchemist, Pride and Prejudice,* Harry Potter series

Favorite college courses: Art Appreciation and Intro to Cultural Anthropology

The person who inspires me the most or whom I would most like to meet: Queen Elizabeth I

Favorite way to relax: With a cup of hot tea and a good book

Your proudest moment or biggest accomplishment: Becoming godmother to my nephew

Favorite food: Green Chile Chicken Enchiladas

Starting college confession: When I first started college, I thought I'd attend for the standard four years just so I could get a degree and a good job. But now I realize college is a place for growing, learning, and discovering. I discovered that I wanted more than a job; I wanted a career. My ideal career would be one in which I would be in a position to help people and have a positive impact on their lives.

I've learned so much from all my classes, and there is still much for me to learn. I've learned so much about myself as well. I now realize that getting involved and making new friends are just as important as "making the grade."

College is not a quick stop in life. It is where you can expand horizons and learn, not just about math and history, but also about yourself. I believe that college is a place where you can figure out who you are and become the person you want to be.

that general education courses are designed to give you the kinds of knowledge and skills you need for the rest of your life. Visit your career center, your library, and the Internet to investigate your interests and learn how to develop and apply them in college and beyond. Talk to your residence hall advisors as well as your professors, academic advisors, and campus chaplains. College is designed to give you all the tools you need to find and achieve your purpose. It's all at your fingertips—but the rest is up to you.

▶ WHERE TO GO FOR **HELP**

On Campus

To find the college support services you need, ask your academic advisor or counselor or consult your college catalog, phone book, and college website. Or call or visit student services (or student affairs). Most of these services are free. In subsequent chapters, we will include a "Where to Go for Help" feature that is specific to the chapter topic.

Academic Advisement Center Help in choosing courses; information on degree requirements.

Academic Skills Center Tutoring; help in study and memory skills; help in studying for exams.

Adult Reentry Center Programs for returning students; supportive contacts with other adult students; information about services such as child care.

Career Center Career library; interest assessments; counseling; help in finding a major; job and internship listings; co-op listings; interviews with prospective employers; help with résumés and interview skills.

Chaplains Worship services; fellowship; personal counseling.

Commuter Services List of off-campus housing, roommate lists, orientation to community, maps, public transportation guides, child-care listings.

Computer Center Minicourses, handouts on campus computer resources.

Counseling Center Confidential counseling for personal concerns, stress management programs.

Disabled Student Services Assistance in overcoming physical barriers or learning disabilities.

Financial Aid and Scholarship Office Information on financial aid programs, scholarships, and grants.

Health Center Help in personal nutrition, weight control, exercise, and sexuality; information on substance abuse programs and other health issues; often includes a pharmacy.

Housing Office Help in locating on- or off-campus housing.

Legal Services Legal aid for students. If your campus has a law school, possible assistance by senior law students.

Math Center Help with math skills.

Physical Education Center Facilities and equipment for exercise and recreational sports.

Writing Center Help with writing assignments.

My Institution's Resources

_____

_____

_____

_____

_____

_____

_____

Managing Your Time and Money

In this chapter YOU WILL LEARN

▶ How to take control of your time and your life

▶ How to use goals and objectives to guide your planning

▶ How to prioritize your use of time

▶ How to combat procrastination

▶ How to organize your day, your week, your school term

▶ The value of a to-do list

▶ How the way you manage time and money may be related

▶ The pros and cons of credit and debit cards

© Gary Gerovac/Masterfile

Jeanne L. Higbee of the University of Minnesota, Twin Cities, contributed her valuable and considerable expertise to the writing of this chapter.

How Do You MANAGE YOUR TIME and MONEY?

A?B?C?A?B?C?A?B?C?

Read the following questions and choose the answer that most fits you:

1 How do you stay in control of your time?

A I religiously schedule my everyday tasks on my calendar or in my handheld personal digital assistant (PDA).

B I sometimes use the task reminder on my cell phone or on my computer.

C I like to keep my options open and prefer not to schedule my time.

2 How do you set academic and personal goals to prioritize your time?

A At the beginning of a term, I schedule my larger academic tasks and then find time for personal activities that help keep me sane.

B I try to keep my academics balanced with my personal goals, but I tend to forget about assignments when there's something to do with my friends.

C I'm not ready to set academic or personal goals right now.

3 What, if anything, distracts you or causes you to procrastinate?

A I never let that happen—I focus on studying by going to a quiet place like the library.

B I try to study in my room with my iPod, but someone always knocks on my door, and I wind up talking to people instead.

C TV shows always draw me in, and so I wind up studying an hour before the test.

4 What does your to-do list look like?

A Very detailed, with everything I expect to accomplish that day—I even schedule meals.

B I usually just write in school stuff and tend to forget about my personal appointments.

C Should I have a list? I usually just do whatever seems right at the time.

5 How do you develop a budget for the term?

A I think about everything that will cost me money during the term and create a budget that I live by.

B I write down a budget, but I occasionally reward myself and buy something I really want.

C I don't live on a budget—I buy whatever I want until I run out of money.

6 How do you use credit cards?

A I have a credit card, but I only charge what I can pay off every month.

B I try to use my credit card wisely, but every now and then I charge more than I should.

C I have more than one credit card, and they're pretty much maxed out. I try when I can to make the minimum payments every month.

Review your responses. **A** responses indicate that you have a good beginning understanding of how to manage your time and money, but you'll still need to work on maintaining those skills. **B** responses indicate that you're doing fairly well with resource management, but there's always room for improvement. **C** responses indicate that you need some help with getting control of your time and money. This course and this book can help you develop the knowledge and skills you need.

How do you approach time? How do you approach money? You might find that you view these important resources differently than your classmates do. Often these differences have to do with your personality and background. And sometimes these differences are so ingrained and automatic that you don't even think about them. For example, if you're a natural organizer, you probably enter all due dates for assignments on your calendar or PDA as soon as you receive each syllabus. If you are careful with your money, you likely adopt and stick to a strict budget. On the other hand, if you take a more laid-back approach to life, you may prefer to be more flexible and go with the flow rather than follow a daily or weekly schedule. You may be good at dealing with the unexpected but also find yourself in trouble because you have wasted either time or money.

How you manage time and money reflects what is most important to you. For instance, if you value friendships above everything else, your academic work might take a back seat to social activities. Or when you can't resist the latest electronic gadget, you might be willing to spend money you don't have.

Taking Control of Your Time

The first step to effective time management is recognizing that *you* can be in control. How often do you find yourself saying "I don't have time"? Once a week? Once a day? Several times a day? The next time you hear yourself saying this, stop and ask whether it is really true. Is it really that you do not have time, or have you chosen, whether consciously or unconsciously, not to make time for that particular task or activity?

Setting Priorities to Achieve Your Goals

Once you have established goals and objectives, decide how you want to prioritize your time. Which goals and objectives are most important to you? Which are the most urgent? For example, studying in order to get a good grade on a test tomorrow may have to take priority over attending a job fair today. Using good time management, you can study during the week prior to the test so that you can attend the job fair the day before. One way that skilled time managers establish priorities is to maintain a to-do list (discussed in more detail later in this chapter)

◀ Some college students have to juggle taking care of children and pursuing a degree.

and then rank the items on that list, determining schedules and deadlines for each task.

Another aspect of setting priorities while in college is finding an appropriate way to balance your academic schedule with the rest of your life. Social activities are an important part of the college experience. Similarly, time alone and time to think are essential to your overall well-being. Of course, for many students the greatest challenge of prioritizing will be balancing school with work and family obligations that are equally important and not optional.

Staying Focused

Many of the decisions you make today are reversible. You may change your major, and your career and life goals may change as well. But the decision to take control of your life—to set your goals and priorities and manage your time accordingly—is an important one. Most first-year students, especially recent high-school graduates, temporarily lose sight of their goals and enjoy their first term of college by opening themselves up to a wide array of new experiences. While we encourage you to do this, within limits, we recognize that some students will spend the next four or five years trying to make up for poor decisions made early in their college careers, decisions that led to plummeting GPAs, the threat of academic probation, or, worse, academic dismissal.

Many students, whether young or old, question the decision to continue in school and may feel temporarily overwhelmed by the additional responsibilities of college. Prioritizing, rethinking some commitments, letting some things go, and weighing the advantages and disadvantages of attending school part-time versus full-time can help you work through this adjustment period. Again, keep your long-term goals in mind and find ways to manage your stress, rather than react to it.

Write • DISCUSS • Compare • Ask • BLOG • Answer • *Journal*

> What is your biggest time-management challenge—is it oversleeping, spending too much time on an online community such as Facebook, juggling work and family responsibilities, or something else?

While this book is full of suggestions for enhancing academic success, the bottom line is staying focused by taking control of your time and your life. Make a plan that begins with your priorities: attending classes, studying, working, spending time with the people who are important to you. Then think about the necessities of life: sleeping, eating, exercising, and relaxing. Leave time for fun things like talking with friends, watching TV, going out for the evening, and relaxing. But finish what needs to be done before you move from work to pleasure. And don't forget about personal

WIRED WINDOW

THE TECHNOLOGY we use daily is a catch-22. On the one hand, technology helps us to be more productive and organize our time efficiently. On the other hand, technology becomes a colossal distraction and a time-waster. College students spend a lot of time chatting online using instant messaging software. Think about how you use instant messaging. How often do you use it while doing something else on the computer? Generally, this kind of multitasking is harmless and often helpful when you are trying to do your "digital errands" like paying bills, buying books, and so on. However, because it is so easy to multi-task, many students also try to do their school work while surfing the web or IMing. Have you ever completed your school work while actively sending and receiving instant messages or while surfing the web? If so, what was the quality of your work? A recent nationwide survey found that over 40 percent of students reported their school work suffered because of multitasking on the web. Are you in that 40 percent? If so, what are some ways that you can disconnect in order to get your work done? One suggestion is to find a quiet study spot and leave your computer in your room. If you can't leave your computer, your room, or your Internet connection, consider purchasing software that will block digital distractions.

time. Depending on your personality and cultural background, you may require more or less time to be alone.

If you live in a residence hall or share an apartment with other college students, communicate with your roommates about how you can coordinate your class schedules so that you each have some privacy. If you live at home with your family, particularly if you are a parent, work together to create special family times as well as quiet study times.

Overcoming Procrastination

Procrastination is a serious problem that can trip up many otherwise capable people. People procrastinate for many reasons. Recent research has found that while about 20 percent of American adults are chronic procrastinators, approximately 70 percent of college students say they typically procrastinate on starting or finishing an assignment. Psychological studies have found that even students who are highly motivated may fear failure, and some even may fear success. Some students procrastinate because they are perfectionists; not doing a task may be easier than having to live up to expectations—either your own or those of your parents, instructors, or peers. Others procrastinate because they find an assigned task boring or irrelevant or consider it "busy work," believing that they can learn the material just as effectively without doing the homework.

Simply not enjoying an assignment is not a good excuse to put it off. Throughout life you'll be faced with tasks that you don't find interesting; in many cases, you won't have the option not to do them. However, procrastinating can signal that it's time to reassess your goals and objectives; maybe you are not ready to make a commitment to academic priorities at this point in your life. Although only you can

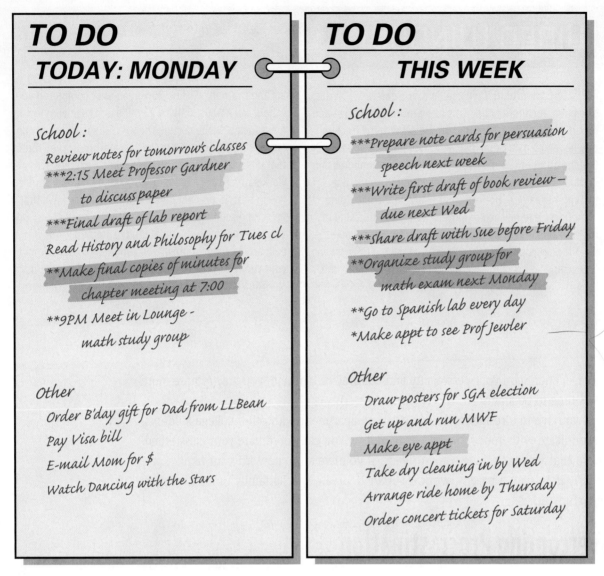

TO DO

TODAY: MONDAY

school:
  Review notes for tomorrow's classes
  ****2:15 Meet Professor Gardner*
     to discuss paper
  ****Final draft of lab report*
  Read History and Philosophy for Tues cl
  ***Make final copies of minutes for*
     chapter meeting at 7:00
  ***9PM Meet in Lounge –*
     math study group

Other
  Order B'day gift for Dad from LLBean
  Pay Visa bill
  E-mail Mom for $
  Watch Dancing with the Stars

TO DO

THIS WEEK

school:
  *****Prepare note cards for persuasion*
     speech next week
  *****Write first draft of book review –*
     due next Wed
  *****share draft with sue before Friday*
  ***Organize study group for*
     math exam next Monday
  ***Go to Spanish lab every day*
  **Make appt to see Prof Jewler*

Other
  Draw posters for SGA election
  Get up and run MWF
  Make eye appt
  Take dry cleaning in by Wed
  Arrange ride home by Thursday
  Order concert tickets for Saturday

▲ **Figure 2.1**   This to-do list won't allow you to forget.

decide, a counselor or academic advisor can help you sort it out. Regardless of its source, procrastination may be your single greatest enemy.

Here are some ways to beat procrastination:

▶ Remind yourself of the possible consequences if you do not get down to work. Then get started.

▶ Create a to-do list (see Figure 2.1). Check off things as you get them done. Review those tasks that aren't getting done. Move them to the top of your next day's list, and make up your mind to do them. Working from a list will give you a feeling of accomplishment and lead you to do more.

▶ Break down big jobs into smaller steps. Tackle short, easy-to-accomplish tasks first.

▶ Promise yourself a reward for finishing the task, such as watching a favorite TV show or going out with friends.

▶ Find a place to study that's comfortable and doesn't allow for distractions and interruptions. Say no to friends and family who want your attention, and agree to spend time with them later at a specific time.

▶ Don't make or take phone calls, text message, e-mail, or surf the web during planned study sessions. If you study in your room, close your door.

Recent research indicates that college students who procrastinate in their studies also avoid confronting other tasks and problems and are more likely to develop unhealthy habits, such as higher alcohol consumption, smoking, insomnia, poor diet, and lack of exercise. If you cannot get procrastination under control, it is in your best interest to seek help at your campus counseling service.

Maintaining a To-Do List

Keeping a to-do list can also help you avoid feeling stressed or out of control. Some people start a new list every day or once a week. Others keep a running list and only throw a page away when everything on the list is done. Use your to-do list to keep track of all the tasks you need to remember, not just academics.

You might include errands you need to run, appointments you need to make, e-mail messages you need to send, and so on. Develop a system for prioritizing the items on your list: highlight; use colored ink; or mark with one, two, or three stars, or *A, B, C.* As you complete each task, cross it off your list. You may be surprised at how much you have accomplished and how good you feel about it.

Making Sure Your Schedule Works For You

As a new student, you may not have had much flexibility in determining your course schedule; by the time you were allowed to register for classes, some sections of the courses you needed may already have been closed. You also may not have known whether you would prefer taking classes back-to-back or giving yourself a break between classes.

Before you register for the next term, consider what kind of schedule will work best for you. If you live on campus, you may want to create a schedule that situates you near a dining hall at mealtimes or forces you to spend breaks between classes at the library. Or you may need breaks in your schedule for relaxation, spending time in a student lounge, college union, or campus center. You might want to avoid returning to your residence hall room to take a nap between classes if the result is feeling lethargic or oversleeping and missing later classes. Be realistic about your personal habits when choosing class times and locations. Also, if you attend a large university, be sure that you allow adequate time to get from building to building.

If you're a commuter student or if you must work off campus to afford college, you may prefer scheduling your classes together in blocks without breaks. Although

block scheduling, which literally means back-to-back classes, allows you to cut travel time by attending school one or two days a week and may provide more flexibility in scheduling employment or family commitments, it can also have significant draw-backs. By attending back-to-back classes, you have little time to process information or to study between classes.

If you become ill on a class day, you could fall behind in all of your classes. Or you may become fatigued sitting in class after class. Block scheduling will make it impossible to have a last-minute study period immediately before a test, since you will be attending another class and are likely to have no more than a fifteen-minute break. Finally, remember that for block-scheduled courses, many exams could be held on the same day. Block scheduling may work better if you can attend lectures at an alternative time in case you are absent and if you seek out instructors who allow you flexibility in completing assignments.

Write • DISCUSS • Compare • Ask • BLOG • Answer • *Journal*

> What do you know about your personal body clock? When during the day or night are you most alert and when do you tend to be tired and unfocused? Is there a time of day when your ability to think and write creatively is at its peak?

Using Schedule Planners

In college, as in life, you will quickly learn that managing time is an important key not only to survival but also to success. A good way to start is to look at the big picture. Use the *term-assignment preview* (Figure 2.2) on pages 23–24 to give yourself an idea of what's ahead. You should complete your term assignment preview by the beginning of the second week of classes so that you can continue to use your time effectively. Then purchase a "week-at-a-glance" planner for the current year. Your campus bookstore may sell one designed just for your school, with important dates and deadlines already provided. You might prefer to use the calendar that comes on your computer, PDA, or cell phone.

Regardless of the format you prefer (electronic or hard copy), enter the notes from your preview sheets into your planner, and continue to enter all due dates as soon as you know them. Write in meeting times and locations, scheduled social events (jot down phone numbers in case something comes up and you need to cancel), study time for each class you're taking, and so forth. Carry your calendar or planner with you in a place where you're not likely to lose it.

The practice of using a daily and weekly planner will become invaluable to you in the world of work. Check your notes daily for the current week and the coming week. Choose a specific time of day to do this, perhaps just before you begin study-ing, before you go to bed, or at a set time on weekends. But check it daily and at the same time of day. It takes just a moment to be certain that you aren't forgetting something important.

	Monday	Tuesday	Wednesday	Thursday	Friday
Week 1					
Week 2					
Week 3					
Week 4					

	Monday	Tuesday	Wednesday	Thursday	Friday
Week 5					
Week 6					
Week 7					
Week 8					

▲ **Figure 2.2** Term Assignment Preview. Using the course syllabi provided by your instructors, enter all due dates on this term calendar. For longer assignments, such as term papers, divide the task into smaller parts and establish your own deadline for each part of the assignment, such as deadlines for choosing a topic, completing your library research, developing an outline of the paper, writing a first draft, and so on.

	Monday	Tuesday	Wednesday	Thursday	Friday
Week 9					
Week 10					
Week 11					
Week 12					

	Monday	Tuesday	Wednesday	Thursday	Friday
Week 13					
Week 14					
Week 15					
Week 16					

▲ **Figure 2.2** (Continued)

Guidelines for Using the Weekly Timetable for Scheduling Week-by-Week

Use Figure 2.3 to tentatively plan how you will spend your hours in a typical week.

▶ Begin by entering all of your commitments for each week—classes, work hours, family commitments, and so on.

▶ Examine your toughest weeks on your term-assignment preview sheet (see Figure 2.2). If paper deadlines and test dates fall during the same week, find time to finish some assignments early to free up study time for tests. Note this in your planner.

▶ Try to reserve at least two hours of study time for each hour spent in class. This two-for-one rule reflects many faculty members' expectations for how much work you should be doing to earn a good grade in their classes. This means that if you are taking a typical full-time class load of fifteen credits, for example, you should be planning to study an additional thirty hours per week. Think of this 45-hour-per-week commitment as comparable to a full-time job. Then if you are also working, reconsider how many hours per week are reasonable for you to be employed above and beyond this commitment, or consider reducing your course load.

▶ Depending on your body clock, obligations, and potential distractions, decide whether you study more effectively in the day, in the evening, or a combination of both. Determine whether you are capable of getting up very early in the morning to study or how late you can stay up at night and still wake up for morning classes.

▶ All assignments are not equal. Estimate how much time you will need for each one, and begin your work early. A good time manager frequently finishes assignments before actual due dates to allow for emergencies.

▶ Keep track of how much time it takes you to complete different kinds of tasks. For example, depending on your skills and interests, it may take longer to read a chapter in a biology text than one in a literature text. Keeping track of your time will help you estimate how much time to allocate for similar tasks in the future. How long does it really take you to complete a set of twenty math problems or to write up a chemistry lab? Using a schedule form like that provided in Figure 2.2 or entering all your activities in your weekly timetable (see Figure 2.3), you can actually track how you spend your time for an entire week.

Organizing Your Day

Being a good student does not necessarily mean studying day and night and doing little else. Keep the following points in mind as you organize your day:

▶ Set realistic goals for your study time. Give yourself adequate time to review, and then test your knowledge when preparing for exams.

▶ Use waiting time (on the bus, before class, waiting for appointments) to review.

▶ Retain what you have learned by allowing time to review as soon as reasonable after class. (Reviewing immediately after class may be possible but not reasonable if you are too burned out to concentrate!)

▶ Know your best times of day to study. Schedule mundane activities, like doing laundry, responding to e-mail, or spending time with friends, for times when it is difficult to concentrate.

	Sunday	Monday	Tuesday	Wednesday	Thursday	Friday	Saturday
6:00							
7:00							
8:00							
9:00							
10:00							
11:00							
12:00							
1:00							
2:00							
3:00							
4:00							
5:00							
6:00							
7:00							
8:00							
9:00							
10:00							
11:00							

▲ **Figure 2.3** Weekly Timetable. This chart has several uses. Using the suggestions in this chapter, create your perfect schedule for next term. Do you want your classes back-to-back or with breaks in between? How early in the morning are you willing to start classes? Do you prefer—or do work or family commitments require you—to take evening classes? Are there times of day when you are more alert? Less alert? How many days per week do you want to attend classes? At some institutions you can go to school full-time by exclusively attending classes on Saturday. Plan how you will spend your time for the coming week. Track all of your activities for a full week by entering into this schedule form everything you do and how much time each task requires. Use this record to help you estimate the time needed for similar activities in the future.

▶ Restrict repetitive, distracting, and time-consuming tasks like checking your e-mail to a certain time, not every hour.

▶ Avoid *multitasking*. Even though you may actually be quite good at it (or at least think that you are), the reality is that you will be able to study more effectively and make better use of your time if you concentrate on one task at a time.

▶ Be flexible. You cannot anticipate every disruption of your plans. Build extra time into your schedule so that unexpected interruptions do not prevent you from meeting your goals.

Don't Overextend Yourself

Being overextended is a primary source of stress for college students. Determine what is a realistic workload for you; this can vary significantly from person to person. Do not take on more than you can handle. Learn to say no. Do not feel obligated to provide a reason; you have the right to decline requests that will prevent you from getting your own work done.

Even with the best intentions, some students who use a time-management plan allow themselves to become overextended. If there is not enough time to carry your course load and meet your commitments, drop a course before the **drop date** so you won't have a low grade on your permanent record. If you receive financial aid, keep in mind that you must be registered for a minimum number of credit hours to be considered a full-time student and so maintain your current level of financial aid.

If dropping a course is not feasible or if other activities are lower on your list of priorities, which is likely for most college students, assess your other time commitments and let go of one or more. Doing so can be very difficult, especially if you think that you are letting other people down. However, it is far preferable to excuse yourself from

▶ **Avoid multitasking so that your study time will be spent effectively.**

an activity in a way that is respectful to others than to fail to come through at the last minute because you have committed to more than you can possibly achieve.

Reduce Distractions

Where should you study? Do not study in places associated with leisure, such as at the kitchen table, in the living room, or in front of the TV, because these lend themselves to interruptions by others and to other distractions. Also, your association with social activities in these locations can distract you even when others are not there. Similarly, it is unwise to study on your bed. You may find yourself drifting off when you need to study, or you may learn to associate your bed with studying and not be able to go to sleep when you need to. Instead find quiet places, both on campus and at home, where you can concentrate and develop a study mind-set each time you sit down to do your work.

Try to stick to a routine as you study. The more firmly you have established a specific time and a quiet place to study, the more effective you will be in keeping up with your schedule. If you have larger blocks of time available on the weekend, for example, take advantage of that time to review or catch up on major projects, such as term papers, that can't be completed effectively in fifty-minute blocks. Break down large tasks and take one thing at a time; then you will make more progress toward your ultimate academic goals.

Here are some more tips to help you deal with distractions:

▶ Turn off the TV, CD player, iPod, DVD, or radio, unless the background noise or music really helps you concentrate on your studies or drowns out more distracting noises (people laughing or talking in other rooms or hallways, for instance).

▶ Don't let personal concerns interfere with studying. If necessary, call a friend or write in a journal before you start to study, and then put your worries away. You might actually put your journal in a drawer and consider that synonymous with putting your problems away.

▶ Develop an agreement with your roommates or family about the need for "quiet hours." If that's not possible, discover a quiet place where you can go to concentrate.

Managing Your Money

Almost all college students have a fixed amount of money available to spend during any given month or term, but sticking to a fixed budget can be tough. Many students overspend their credit cards, and some get so overextended that they have to drop out of college and work to pay their debts.

National surveys have found that most college students worry about paying for college. Although some students have scholarships, financial aid, or parents who pay for their education, others must work to pay for tuition and living expenses. For many students, graduating from college is a goal they can reach only with careful financial planning.

Confessions of a College Student

Name: Drew Trimble

Age: 19

University: University of Kentucky

Hometown: Van Lear, Kentucky

Major: Political Science and Communication

Favorite book(s): *Brave New World, The Fred Factor, Angels and Demons*

Favorite college course: Communication 101, Introduction to Communication

The person who inspires me the most or whom I would most like to meet: Job of the Bible, a virtuous and kind man, who was subjected to a life of misery—everything the devil could throw at him—and emerged victorious.

Favorite way to relax: Sitting on front porches; running.

Your proudest moment or biggest accomplishment: My proudest moment occurred when a wrestler I trained who became like a brother to me won the Kentucky Middle School State Wrestling Championship.

Favorite food: Jolly Rancher Jelly Beans

Money management confession: I learned how to manage money from the mistakes of a friend, who was a compulsive shopper. When we ate lunch together, I noticed that she always put the bill on her credit card. At the mall she would put her numerous purchases on her card without even thinking. When I finally asked her where she got the money to pay for the food, clothes, and trips that she indulged in, she told me that she was thousands of dollars in debt and hoped someday to have a job that would allow her to pay it all off. When I heard this, I convinced her to allow me to take her credit card and keep it in a safe place, and I promised myself never to let my credit get out of control. The good news is that she received some help from a family member, never asked me to return her card, and changed her spending habits. She is now a spokesperson for a major credit card company. It's funny how things work out.

Developing a Budget

To develop a budget, you need to understand how much income you can count on and your spending habits. In college you will have many expenses that recur at regular intervals, such as tuition, books, fees, and room and board. But other expenses, such as the costs of entertainment and clothes, are difficult to track. It is easy to get to the end of the month and realize that you have no idea where your money went. That's why it is important that you develop a system for tracking your income and your expenses. That information will help you create an accurate budget to guide your spending.

Credit Cards, Debit Cards, and College

Many college students almost never write checks or pay for anything in cash. Instead, they use either credit or debit cards. While using these cards can make money management easier, you'll need to use them wisely in order to avoid financial trouble.

Write • DISCUSS • Compare • Ask • BLOG • Answer • *Journal*

> Do you have a credit card? If not, what prevents you from getting one? If you do have a card (or cards), do you feel that you're in control of the way you use it? Why or why not?

Using a credit card is often viewed as an effective way to establish a positive credit history. But don't hold more credit cards than you can afford. A good rule of thumb is to not have more credit available to you than you can pay off in two months.

By using a debit card rather than credit cards, you restrict your spending to the amount of money in your bank account. However, since a debit card provides ready access to your bank account, it's important for you to keep your card in a safe place away from your personal identification number (PIN). The safest way to protect your account is to commit your PIN to memory.

▷ WHERE TO GO FOR HELP

On Campus

Academic Skills Center Along with assistance on studying for exams, reading textbooks, and taking notes, your campus academic skills center has specialists in time management who can offer advice for your specific problems.

Your Academic Advisor/Counselor If you have a good relationship with this person, he or she may be able to offer advice or to refer you to another person on campus, including those in the offices mentioned above.

A Fellow Student A friend and good student who is willing to help you with time management can be one of your most valuable resources in this area.

Your Institution's Financial Aid Office Professionals in this office will help you understand financial aid opportunities and how to apply for scholarships.

Campus Programs Be on the lookout for special campus programs on money management.

Online

Dartmouth College Academic Skills Center http://www.dartmouth.edu/~acskills/success/time.html. This website offers tips and resources for managing your time. Under "Time Management Resources," click to view the Time Management Video. You will need QuickTime for this; it can be downloaded free from the QuickTime website.

University of Iowa, Office of Financial Aid http://www.uiowa.edu/financial-aid/managing/college.html. This website offers help with managing your money while you're in college.

Discovering How You Learn: A Primer for Lifelong Learning

In this chapter YOU WILL LEARN

▶ Different approaches to understanding your learning styles or preferences

▶ How learning styles and teaching styles may differ

▶ How to optimize your learning style in any classroom setting

▶ How to understand and recognize a learning disability

© Sam Pellissier/SuperStock

How Do You LEARN?

A?B?C?A?B?C?A?B?C?

Read the following questions and choose the answer that most fits you.

1 **Do you know whether you learn better by seeing, hearing, reading, or working with your hands?**

(A) I haven't ever thought about this.

(B) Yes, I learned about my preferred learning style in another class.

(C) I think I know how I learn best, but I'm not really sure.

2 **Have you ever heard of the theory of multiple intelligences?**

(A) No, never. What does that do?

(B) Yes, I've completed a multiple intelligences survey before, and I know the areas of intelligence where I am strongest.

(C) Is it the same as the theory that tells you about musical and bodily intelligence? Then, maybe I do.

3 **Do you know how to utilize your learning style to do well in any class you take?**

(A) I really don't know what you're talking about.

(B) I know my own preferred learning style, but so far I've been able to adapt to any instructor and classroom situation.

(C) I know I don't learn well in big lecture classes. I'd much rather be in small classes where there is a lot of discussion. I really don't know exactly how I can learn in a big class where all I do is listen and take notes.

4 **If you were having trouble in your courses, especially with reading and taking exams, where would you go for help?**

(A) I'm too stubborn to get help—I'd probably fail first.

(B) I would visit the learning center on my campus to see whether experts who work there could help me.

(C) I might see my advisor or just tell my parents about it, but I'm not sure what else I would do.

5 **Do some of your courses require you to learn in different ways?**

(A) I never thought about it—I just go to class and take notes. I never do anything differently.

(B) Yes, definitely. Science and education courses use more hands-on learning. English and history courses are usually discussion or lecture style.

(C) I guess so—for some classes I only take notes; for others I participate in discussion.

Review your responses. (A) responses indicate that you haven't really thought about how you learn. This chapter will help you discover how to think about your learning strengths and preferences. (B) responses indicate that you have already thought clearly about how you learn best. You'll be able to increase your knowledge as you look at learning in different ways. (C) responses indicate that you are somewhat familiar with the idea of learning styles, but you can definitely benefit from more information so that you'll have a better idea of how you learn most effectively.

People learn differently. This is hardly a novel idea, but in order for you to do well in college it is important that you become aware of your preferred way or style of learning. Experts agree that there is no one best way to learn.

You may have trouble paying attention to a long lecture, or listening may be the way you learn best. You may love classroom discussion, or you may consider hearing what other students have to say in class a big waste of time.

Write • DISCUSS • Compare • Ask • BLOG • Answer • *Journal*

How do you like to learn? Do you like classroom discussion with your fellow students or do you prefer a lecture-type situation?

You've probably already discovered that college instructors and even courses have their own inherent styles. Many instructors rely almost solely on lecturing while others use lots of visual aids (such as PowerPoint outlines, charts, graphs, and pictures) to convey information. In science courses, you will conduct experiments or go on field trips where you can observe or touch what you are studying; in dance, theater, or physical education, learning takes place in both your body and your mind. And in almost all courses, you'll also learn by reading textbooks and other materials.

Some instructors are friendly and warm; others seem to want little interaction with students. It's safe to say that in at least some of your college courses, you won't find a close match between the way you learn most effectively and the way you're being taught. This chapter will help you first to understand how you learn best, and then to think of ways you can create a link between your style of learning and the expectations of each course and each instructor.

There are many ways of thinking about and describing **learning styles**. Some of these will make a lot of sense to you; others may initially seem confusing or counterintuitive. Some learning styles theories are very simple, with only two or three components, and others are far more complex.

One of the simplest descriptions of learning styles is the division of all learners into *splitters* and *lumpers*. You are a splitter if you tend to analyze information logically and break it down into small parts and a lumper if you tend to watch for patterns and relationships in order to get the big picture.[1] Differences between splitters and lumpers are often played out in the biological sciences. In biology, lumpers are researchers who prefer to take a broad view and assume that differences between species are not as important as their similarities. Splitters, on the other hand, use very precise definitions and create new categories and subcategories to account for every difference.

Write • DISCUSS • Compare • Ask • BLOG • Answer • *Journal*

> Are you a splitter or a lumper? Blog about how you would categorize yourself and why.

In addition to its focus on learning styles, this chapter will also explore **learning disabilities**. You may know someone who has been diagnosed with a learning disability, such as dyslexia or attention deficit disorder. By reading this chapter you will learn more about common types of learning disabilities, how to recognize them, and what to do if you or someone you know has a learning disability.

---

[1] P. Kirby, "Cognitive Style, Learning Style and Transfer Skill Acquisition," *Information Series* 195 (Columbus, OH: Ohio State University, National Center for Research in Vocational Education, 1979).

Learning About Learning Styles

Of the dozens of learning style models, we will review two that are well-known and relevant to your own learning style.

▶ Multiple Intelligences

▶ The VARK (Visual, Aural, Read/Write, Kinesthetic) Learning Styles Inventory

You will notice some overlap between different learning style models, but using more than one of them may help you do a more precise job of discovering your learning style. If you are interested in reading more about learning styles, your library and your learning center will have many resources available to you.

Multiple Intelligences

One way of measuring how people learn uses the theory of multiple intelligences, developed in 1983 by Howard Gardner, a professor of education at Harvard University. Gardner's theory is based on the premise that the traditional notion of human intelligence is very limited. He proposes eight different intelligences to describe how humans learn.

As you might imagine, Gardner's work is very controversial since it calls into question the limitations of traditional verbal-linguistic and logical-mathematical definitions of intelligence. Gardner argues that students should be encouraged to develop the abilities they have and that evaluation should measure all forms of intelligence.

As you think of yourself and your friends, what kinds of intelligences do you have? Do college courses measure all the ways that you are intelligent? Here is a short inventory that will help you recognize your multiple intelligences.

Multiple Intelligences Inventory

According to Gardner, all human beings have at least eight different types of intelligence. Depending on your background and age, some intelligences are likely to be more developed than others. This activity will help you find out what your intelligences are. Knowing this, you can work to strengthen the other intelligences that you do not use as often. Put a check mark next to the items that apply to you.

Verbal/Linguistic Intelligence

_____ I enjoy telling stories and jokes.
_____ I enjoy word games (for example, *Scrabble* and puzzles).
_____ I am a good speller (most of the time).
_____ I like talking and writing about my ideas.
_____ If something breaks and won't work, I read the instruction book before I try to fix it.
_____ When I work with others in a group presentation, I prefer to do the writing and library research.

Visual/Spatial Intelligence

_____ I prefer a map to written directions.
_____ I enjoy hobbies such as photography.
_____ I like to doodle on paper whenever I can.
_____ In a magazine, I prefer looking at the pictures rather than reading the text.
_____ If something breaks and won't work, I tend to study the diagram of how it works.

Musical/Rhythmic Intelligence

_____ I enjoy listening to CDs and the radio.
_____ I like to sing.
_____ I like to have music playing when doing homework or studying.
_____ I can remember the melodies of many songs.
_____ If something breaks and won't work, I tend to tap my fingers to a beat while I figure it out.

Logical/Mathematical Intelligence

_____ I really enjoy my math class.
_____ I like to find out how things work.
_____ I enjoy computer and math games.
_____ I love playing chess, checkers, or Monopoly.
_____ If something breaks and won't work, I look at the pieces and try to figure out how it works.

Bodily/Kinesthetic Intelligence

_____ My favorite class is gym because I like sports.
_____ When looking at things, I like touching them.
_____ I use a lot of body movements when talking.
_____ I tend to tap my fingers or play with my pencil during class.
_____ If something breaks and won't work, I tend to play with the pieces to try to fit them together.

Interpersonal Intelligence

_____ I get along well with others.
_____ I have several very close friends.
_____ I like working with others in groups.
_____ Friends ask my advice because I seem to be a natural leader.
_____ If something breaks and won't work, I try to find someone who can help me.

Source: www.ldrc.ca/projects/miinventory/mitest.html.

Intrapersonal Intelligence

_____ I like to work alone without anyone bothering me.

_____ I don't like crowds.

_____ I know my own strengths and weaknesses.

_____ I find that I am strong-willed, independent, and don't follow the crowd.

_____ If something breaks and won't work, I wonder whether it's worth fixing.

Naturalist Intelligence

_____ I am keenly aware of my surroundings and of what goes on around me.

_____ I like to collect things like rocks, sports cards, and stamps.

_____ I like to get away from the city and enjoy nature.

_____ I enjoy learning the names of living things in the environment, such as flowers and trees.

_____ If something breaks down, I look around me to try and see what I can find to fix the problem.

A verbal/linguistic learner likes to read, write, and tell stories and is good at memorizing information. A logical/mathematical learner likes to work with numbers and is good at problem-solving and logical processes. A visual/spatial learner likes to draw and play with machines and is good at puzzles and reading maps and charts. A bodily/kinesthetic learner likes to move around and is good at sports, dance, and acting. A musical/rhythmic learner likes to sing and play an instrument and is good at remembering melodies and noticing pitches and rhythms. An interpersonal learner likes to have many friends and is good at understanding people, leading others, and mediating conflicts. Intrapersonal learners like to work alone, understand themselves well, and are original thinkers. A naturalistic learner likes to be outside and is good at preservation, conservation, and organizing a living area.

You can use your intelligences to help you make decisions about a major, choose activities, and investigate career options. Which of these eight intelligences best describes you?

TOTAL SCORE

_____ Verbal/Linguistic	_____ Musical/Rhythmic
_____ Logical/Mathematical	_____ Interpersonal
_____ Visual/Spatial	_____ Intrapersonal
_____ Bodily/Kinesthetic	_____ Naturalist

Add the number of check marks you made in each section. Your score for each intelligence will be a number between 1 and 10. Note your high scores of 7 or more in order to get a sense of your own multiple intelligences.

Write • DISCUSS • Compare • Ask • BLOG • Answer • _Journal_

Do you agree with Howard Gardner that these are the eight styles of learning? Why or why not?

The VARK (Visual, Aural, Read/Write, and Kinesthetic) Learning Styles Inventory

The VARK system is different from other learning styles theories because it relies less on basic personality or intelligence and more on *how learners prefer to use their senses to learn.* The acronym VARK stands for visual, aural, read/write, and kinesthetic. Visual learners prefer to learn information through charts, graphs, symbols, and other visual means. Aural learners prefer to hear information. Read/write learners prefer to learn information that is displayed as words, and kinesthetic learners prefer to learn through experience and practice, whether simulated or real. To determine your learning style according to the VARK inventory, respond to the questionnaire below.

The VARK Questionnaire

Version 7.0

This questionnaire is designed to tell you something about your preferences in the way you work with information. Choose the answer that best explains your preference. Check the box next to that item. Please select all the boxes that apply to you. If none of the response options applies to you, leave the item blank.

1. You are helping someone who wants to go to your airport, town center, or railway station. You would:
   - ☐ a. go with her.
   - ☐ b. tell her the directions.
   - ☐ c. write down the directions (without a map).
   - ☐ d. draw, or give her a map.

2. You are not sure whether a word should be spelled "dependent" or "dependant." You would:
   - ☐ a. see the words in your mind and choose by the way they look.
   - ☐ b. think about how each word sounds and choose one.
   - ☐ c. find it in a dictionary.
   - ☐ d. write both words on paper and choose one.

3. You are planning a holiday for a group. You want some feedback from them about the plan. You would:
   - ☐ a. describe some of the highlights.
   - ☐ b. use a map or website to show them the places.
   - ☐ c. give them a copy of the printed itinerary.
   - ☐ d. phone, text, or e-mail them.

4. You are going to cook something as a special treat for your family. You would:
   - ☐ a. cook something you know without the need for instructions.
   - ☐ b. ask friends for suggestions.
   - ☐ c. look through the cookbook for ideas from the pictures.
   - ☐ d. use a cookbook where you know there is a good recipe.

5. A group of tourists wants to learn about the parks or wildlife reserves in your area. You would:
   - ☐ a. talk, or arrange a talk for them, about parks or wildlife reserves.
   - ☐ b. show them Internet pictures, photographs, or picture books.
   - ☐ c. take them to a park or wildlife reserve and walk with them.
   - ☐ d. give them a book or pamphlets about the parks or wildlife reserves.

6. You are about to purchase a digital camera or mobile phone. Other than price, what would most influence your decision?
   - ☐ a. Trying or testing it.
   - ☐ b. Reading the details about its features.
   - ☐ c. It is a modern design and looks good.
   - ☐ d. The salesperson telling me about its features.

7. Remember a time when you learned how to do something new. Try to avoid choosing a physical skill, (e.g., riding a bike). You learned best by:
   - ☐ a. watching a demonstration.
   - ☐ b. listening to somebody explaining it and then asking questions.
   - ☐ c. diagrams and charts–visual clues.
   - ☐ d. written instructions–e.g., a manual or textbook.

8. You have a problem with your knee. You would prefer that the doctor:
   - ☐ a. give you a web address or something to read about it.
   - ☐ b. use a plastic model of a knee to show what is wrong.
   - ☐ c. describe what is wrong.
   - ☐ d. show you a diagram of what is wrong.

9. You want to learn a new program, skill, or game on a computer. You would:
   - ☐ a. read the written instructions that came with the program.
   - ☐ b. talk with people who know about the program.
   - ☐ c. use the controls or keyboard.
   - ☐ d. follow the diagrams in the book that came with it.

10. I like websites that have:
    - ☐ a. things I can click on or try.
    - ☐ b. interesting design and visual features.
    - ☐ c. interesting written descriptions, lists, and explanations.
    - ☐ d. audio channels where I can hear music, radio programs, or interviews.

11. Other than price, what would most influence your decision to buy a new nonfiction book?
    - ☐ a. The appealing way it looks.
    - ☐ b. Quickly reading parts of it.
    - ☐ c. A friend talks about it and recommends it.
    - ☐ d. It has real-life stories, experiences, and examples.

12. You are using a book, CD, or website to learn how to take photos with your new digital camera. You would like to have:
    - ☐ a. a chance to ask questions and talk about the camera and its features.
    - ☐ b. clear written instructions, with lists and bullet points about what to do.
    - ☐ c. diagrams showing the camera and what each part does.
    - ☐ d. many examples of good and poor photos and how to improve them.

13. You prefer a teacher or a presenter who uses:
    - ☐ a. demonstrations, models, or practical sessions.
    - ☐ b. question and answer, talk, group discussion, or guest speakers.
    - ☐ c. handouts, books, or readings.
    - ☐ d. diagrams, charts, or graphs.

14. You have finished a competition or test and would like some feedback. You would like to have feedback:
    - ☐ a. using examples from what you have done.
    - ☐ b. using a written description of your results.
    - ☐ c. from somebody who talks your work through with you.
    - ☐ d. using graphs showing what you achieved.

15. You are going to choose food at a restaurant or café. You would:
    - ☐ a. choose something you have had there before.
    - ☐ b. listen to the waiter or ask friends to recommend choices.
    - ☐ c. choose from descriptions in the menu.
    - ☐ d. look at what others are eating or at pictures of each dish.

16. You have to make an important speech at a conference or special occasion. You would:
    - ☐ a. make diagrams or get graphs to help explain things.
    - ☐ b. write a few key words and practice saying your speech over and over.
    - ☐ c. write out your speech and learn from reading it over several times.
    - ☐ d. gather many examples and stories to make the talk real and practical.

Source: www.vark-learn.com/english/index.asp.

Scoring the VARK

Use the following scoring chart to find the VARK category to which each of your answers corresponds. Circle the letters that correspond to your answers. For example, if you answered b and c for question 3, circle V and R in the question 3 row.

Question	A category	B category	C category	D category
3	K	V	R	A

Scoring Chart

Question	A category	B category	C category	D category
1	K	A	R	V
2	V	A	R	K
3	K	V	R	A
4	K	A	V	R
5	A	V	K	R
6	K	R	V	A
7	K	A	V	R
8	R	K	A	V
9	R	A	K	V
10	K	V	R	A
11	V	R	A	K
12	A	R	V	K
13	K	A	R	V
14	K	R	A	V
15	K	A	R	V
16	V	A	R	K

Count the number of each of the VARK letters you have circled to get your score for each VARK category.

Total number of **V**s circled =_____

Total number of **A**s circled =_____

Total number of **R**s circled =_____

Total number of **K**s circled =_____

Scoring VARK

Because you could choose more than one answer for each question, the scoring is not just a simple matter of counting. It is like four stepping stones across some water. Enter your scores from *highest* **to** *lowest* on the stones below, with their V, A, R, and K labels.

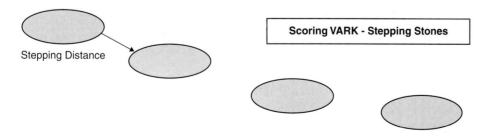

Stepping Distance

Scoring VARK - Stepping Stones

Your stepping distance comes from this table.

The total of my four VARK scores is -	My stepping distance is
16–21	1
22–27	2
28–32	3
More than 32	4

Follow these steps to establish your preferences.

1. Your first preference is always your highest score. Check that first stone as one of your preferences.

2. Now subtract your second highest score from your first. If that figure is larger than your stepping distance, you have a single preference. Otherwise, check this stone as another preference and continue with step 3 below.

3. Subtract your third score from your second one. If that figure is larger than your stepping distance, you have a bimodal preference. If not, check your third stone as a preference and continue with step 4 below.

4. Lastly, subtract your fourth score from your third one. If that figure is larger than your stepping distance, you have a trimodal preference. Otherwise, check your fourth stone as a preference, and you have all four modes as your preferences.

Note: If you are bimodal, trimodal, or have checked all four modes as your preferences, you can be described as multimodal in your VARK preferences.

Write • DISCUSS • Compare • Ask • BLOG • Answer • *Journal*

Did your VARK score surprise you at all? Did you know what type of learner you were before taking the test? If so, when did you discover this? How do you use your modality to your benefit?

Using VARK Results to Study More Effectively

How can knowing your VARK score help you do better in your college classes? Here are ways of using learning styles to develop your own study strategies:

▶ If you have a visual learning preference, underline or highlight your notes, use symbols, charts, or graphs to display your notes, use different arrangements of words on the page, and redraw your pages from memory.

▶ If you are an aural learner, talk with others to verify the accuracy of your lecture notes. Put your notes on a CD and listen or record class lectures. Read your notes out loud; ask yourself questions and speak your answers.

WIRED WINDOW

IF YOU SCORED an aural, visual, or read/write preference on the VARK, you can use technology to enhance how you learn course material. Students with an aural preference can use a digital recorder or micro-cassette recorder to record lectures and then listen to them again later. If you have an iPod, you can purchase a microphone attachment that allows you to use the iPod as a digital audio recorder. Make sure that you have your professors' permissions to record their lectures. In addition to recording lectures, you can find supplemental course material through podcasts and via iTunes. A number of colleges and universities provide podcasts for many of their courses for free on iTunes. You can browse through course offerings in the iTunesU section or you can search for a term in the iTunes store and limit it to iTunesU results. Try searching the web to find podcasts and audio files to help you enhance your knowledge of a certain topic. (Hint: Try searching for a specific subject and the word "podcast." For instance, you might search "Introduction to Philosophy podcast.") Once you have found the podcasts, you can download them in the sequence arranged by the podcaster or download the ones that will supplement material for your course. As with other digital files, create a filing system that allows you to find them easily on your iPod or your computer when you need to review the material again later.

▶ If you have a read/write learning preference, write and rewrite your notes and read your notes silently. Organize diagrams or flow charts into statements, write imaginary exam questions, and respond in writing.

▶ If you are a kinesthetic learner, you will need to use all your senses in learning—sight, touch, taste, smell, and hearing. Supplement your notes with real-world examples; move and gesture while you are reading or speaking your notes.

When Learning Styles and Teaching Styles Are in Conflict

Researchers have found that college instructors tend to teach in ways that conform to their own particular style of learning. So if you have an instructor who learns best in a read/write mode or aural mode, it is probable that her class will be primarily a lecture-only experience with little opportunity for either interaction or visual and kinesthetic learning.

Conversely, an instructor who himself needs a more interactive, hands-on classroom environment will likely involve students in classroom discussion and learning through experience.

When you recognize a mismatch between how you learn best and how you are being taught, it is important that you take more control over your learning process. Don't depend on the instructor or the classroom environment to give you everything you need to maximize your learning. Employ your own unique preferences, talents, and abilities in developing ways to study and retain information. Look back through this chapter to remind yourself of the ways that you can use your own learning styles to be more successful in any class you take.

Confessions of a College Student

Name: Cristina B. Jimenez

Age: 27

College: Pima Community College

Hometown: Nogales Sonora, Mexico

Major: Education

Favorite books(s): *The Wretched of the Earth, Since Predator Came, Fantasies of the Master Race*

Favorite college course: American Heritage

The person who inspires me the most or whom I would most like to meet: Ward Churchill; he is an inspiration to all of us who share Native American heritage.

Heroes: My heroes are all of those people who struggle every day to survive, including those living on a reservation in extreme poverty who yet are happy and accomplish their goals.

Favorite way to relax: Running and playing with my dog.

Are you the first to go to college in your family? If so, what impact has that had on your experience? I am the first person to go to college in my family and am a positive influence on my nephews and nieces.

Favorite food: I am a vegan, which means I do not eat animals or animal-derivative products.

My learning styles confession: I have two types of learning styles; I am a visual learner and a kinesthetic, according to the situation. I learn more when information is provided through graphics, PowerPoint presentations, or any other visual aids. This system works better for me in class. However, I also find myself a kinesthetic learner because when I study for a test I need to divide my time between twenty minutes of studying and ten minutes of either watching television or listening to music. This helps me retain more information.

Learning with a Learning Disability

While everyone has a learning style, a portion of the population has what is characterized as a learning disability (LD). Learning disabilities are usually recognized and diagnosed in grade school. But occasionally students are very successful at compensating for a learning problem and reach college never having been properly diagnosed or assisted.

What Is a Learning Disability?

A learning disability is a disorder that affects people's ability either to interpret what they see and hear or to link information from different parts of the brain. These limitations can show up as specific difficulties with spoken and written language, coordination, self-control, or attention. Such difficulties can impede learning to read, write, or do math. LD is a broad term that covers a number of possible causes, symptoms, treatments, and outcomes. Because of this, it is difficult to diagnose or to pinpoint the causes. The types of LD that most commonly affect college students are academic skill disorders, including developmental reading, writing, and mathematics disorders.

Dyslexia, a developmental reading disorder, is quite widespread. A person can have problems with any of the tasks involved in reading. However, scientists have found that a significant number of people with dyslexia share an inability to distinguish or separate the sounds in spoken words. For instance, dyslexic individuals sometimes have difficulty assigning the appropriate sounds to letters either by themselves or when letters are combined to form words. However, there is more to reading than recognizing words. If the brain is unable to form images or relate new ideas to those stored in memory, the reader can't understand or remember the new concepts. So other types of reading disabilities can appear when the focus of reading shifts from word identification to comprehension.

Writing, too, involves several brain areas and functions. The brain networks for vocabulary, grammar, hand movement, and memory must all be in good working order. So a *developmental writing disorder* may result from problems in any of these areas. Someone who can't distinguish the sequence of sounds in a word will often have problems with spelling. Persons with writing disabilities, particularly *expressive language disorders* (the inability to express oneself using accurate language or sentence structure), are often unable to compose complete grammatical sentences.

A student with a *developmental arithmetic disorder* will have difficulty recognizing numbers and symbols, memorizing facts such as the multiplication table, aligning numbers, and understanding abstract concepts like place value and fractions.

Another common type of learning disability is an *attention disorder*. Some students who have attention disorders appear to daydream excessively. And once you get their attention, they may be easily distracted. Individuals with either attention deficit disorder (ADD) or attention deficit hyperactivity disorder (ADHD) often have trouble organizing tasks or completing their work. They don't seem to listen to or follow directions. Their work may be messy and appear careless. Attention disorders, with or without hyperactivity, are not considered learning disabilities in themselves. However, because attention problems can seriously interfere with academic performance, they often accompany academic skill disorders.

Here are some additional warning signs that will help you determine whether you or someone you know has a learning disability.

▶ Do you perform poorly on tests even when you feel you have studied and are capable of performing better?

▶ Do you have trouble spelling words?

▶ Do you work harder than your fellow classmates at basic reading and writing?

▶ Do your instructors tell you that your performance in class is "inconsistent"? For example, do you answer questions correctly in class but have trouble writing your answers?

▶ Do you have a really short attention span, or do your parents or instructors say that you do things "without thinking"?

Responding yes to any of the above questions *does not necessarily* mean that you have a learning disability. However, if you are concerned, you can use the resources of your campus's learning center, office for students with special needs, or student disabilities office to help you respond to any problem you have and devise ways to learn more effectively. And anyone who is diagnosed with a learning disability is in very good company. Magic Johnson, Jay Leno, Whoopi Goldberg, Tom Cruise, Cher, and Danny Glover are just a few of the famous and successful people who have been diagnosed with learning disabilities. A final word: A learning disability is a *learning difference*, but it is in no way related to intelligence.

Having a learning disability is not a sign that you are "dumb." Far from it! Some of the most intelligent individuals in human history have had a learning disability.

▶ **Anyone can have a learning disability.**

WHERE TO GO FOR **HELP**

On Campus

To learn more about learning styles and learning disabilities, talk to your first-year seminar instructor about campus resources. Most campuses will have a learning center or center for students with disabilities. You may also find that instructors within the area of education or psychology have a strong interest in the processes of learning. Finally, don't forget your library or the Internet. A great deal of published information is available to describe how people learn.

Books

Hallowell, Edward M. (foreword), Jonathan Mooney, and David Cole. *Learning Outside the Lines: Two Ivy League Students with Learning Disabilities and ADHD Give You the Tools for Academic Success and Educational Revolution.* New York: Fireside, 2000.

Nadeau, Kathleen G. *Survival Guide for College Students with ADD or LD.* Washington, DC: Magination, 2006.

Quinn, Patricia O., MD, ed. *ADD and the College Student: A Guide for High School and College Students*

with Attention Deficit Disorder. Washington, DC: Magination, 2001.

Online

LD Pride http://www.ldpride.net/learningstyles.MI.htm. This site was developed in 1998 by Liz Bogod, an adult with learning disabilities. It provides general information about learning styles and learning disabilities and offers an interactive diagnostic tool to determine your learning style.

Support 4 Learning http://www.support4learning .org.uk/education/learning_styles.cfm. This site is supported by HERO, Higher Education and Research Opportunities, which is the official online gateway to United Kingdom (UK) universities, colleges, and research organizations. The site provides learning style inventories and helpful hints about how to use your learning style to do well in college courses.

National Center for Learning Disabilities http:// www.ncld.org. This is the official website of the National Center for Learning Disabilities. The site provides a variety of resources on diagnosing and understanding learning disabilities.

Majors and Careers: Making the Right Choice

In this chapter YOU WILL LEARN

▶ Tips for thriving in the current economy

▶ How majors, interests, and careers are linked—but not always

▶ How to plan a career itinerary for each year of college

▶ The skills employers seek in college graduates

▶ How to search for a job

© Lester Lefkowitz/CORBIS

Philip Gardner of Michigan State University contributed his valuable and considerable expertise to the writing of this chapter.

What Do You Know ABOUT YOUR MAJOR and INTENDED CAREER?

A?B?C?A?B?C?A?B?C?

Check the items below that apply to you:

1 *Do you plan to visit your campus's career center or your career advisor?*

A I will so they can help me prepare for what I'll need to do to meet my goals after graduation.

B I've thought about it, but I'm a little nervous because I'm not really sure I know what I want to do.

C No—I already know what job I want. I don't see how they can help me.

2 *Do you think it would be a good idea to work while you're in college?*

A If I could find a job on campus or a part-time job that relates to my major, it would be a good idea.

B I'm not sure. I could use some extra money, but I don't know what kind of job to look for.

C I'd rather not work; that will cut into my social life. But if I have to work, I want a job that will pay me a lot of money.

3 *Why is networking important in deciding on and advancing in a career?*

A If I make connections with people who are doing what I think I want to do, I can learn more about the job and maybe have an "in" on a future job.

B I know networking is important, but I always feel funny about introducing myself to someone I don't know.

C Networking is important because success is all about whom you know, not what you know. My motto is "Fake it and make it."

4 *What kinds of questions are good to ask during an interview for a job?*

A I like to ask what the work environment is like to determine whether I would like to work there.

B I usually just let them ask me all the questions—I can never think of anything to ask.

C Mostly I want to know how much vacation and sick leave I would get.

5 *How did you decide on, or how do you plan to choose, your major?*

A I have thought about both my personal interests and what the job market is offering in the way of my interests.

B I am getting a handle on what my interests are by taking a wide range of courses, but beyond that I haven't thought much about a major.

C I guess I'll just major in whatever kinds of courses I get the best grades in.

Review your responses. **A** responses indicate that you are already making plans while you're in college for what you'll do when you graduate. **B** responses indicate that you're beginning to think about the links between college and career, but you're not doing everything you could. **C** responses indicate that you're not taking the link between college and career very seriously. However you responded, this chapter will offer you important information about how your college education can prepare you for the future.

Students come to college for many reasons, but for many a central purpose of college is gaining the knowledge and skills necessary for future employment. Your success in your work life will often depend on whether the profession or career you think you want to pursue is really right for you. But sometimes success in the workplace depends on your ability to do simple things well, such as being on time, being honest, and doing your best. Let's look at the work experiences of two college students, Sara and John.

Sara entered college with thoughts of majoring in the sciences because she enjoyed working in the laboratory at her hometown hospital. Her concern for helping others led her to choose nursing as a major; it was a good career path that combined her two primary interests. Sara sailed through the first two years, excelling in her science classes. During her junior year, she began her nursing courses and spent time observing nursing practice in her university's teaching hospital. After a summer working in various departments of her hometown hospital, Sara made an appointment with a career counselor. She confessed that she did not like being around sick people every day and wanted to change her major but had no idea of what she wanted to do. Sara was wise to change her major before she began what would have been a frustrating career as a nurse.

John explored several majors during his first two years in college by choosing his elective courses with careers in mind and talking to his friends. He settled on business as a major, focusing on finance. John had high aspirations of working for a Fortune 500 company and earning a six-figure salary within five years of graduation. He performed above average in his academic work, although he was occasionally slack with assignments and frequently missed classes. He interned with two prominent companies and eventually accepted a position at a Fortune 500 company. To his surprise, he was laid off nine months later because he was frequently late for work and missed important deadlines on two occasions. Although John had high aspirations while he was in college, he somehow never learned or took seriously the basic habits of career success.

Like Sara and John, students planning for careers frequently encounter bumps along the way. Choosing a career is a process of discovery, involving a willingness to remain open to new ideas and experiences. Why begin thinking about your career now? Because many of the decisions you make during your first year in college will have an impact on where you end up after you graduate.

Careers and the New Economy

In your lifetime, companies have restructured and taken on new shapes to remain competitive. As a result, major changes have taken place in how we work, where we work, and the ways we prepare for work while in college. The following characteristics define today's economy:

▶ **Global.** Increasingly, national companies have gone multinational, not only moving into overseas markets but seeking cheaper labor, capital, and resources abroad. Factories around the world built to similar standards can turn out essentially the same products. Your career is bound to be affected by the global economy, even if you never leave the United States. For example, when you call an 800 number for customer service, the person who talks to you might be answering your call in Iowa, Ireland, or India. In his recent best-selling book, *The World Is Flat*, Thomas Friedman reminds his readers that talent has become more important than geography in determining a person's opportunity in life. College graduates in the U.S. are now competing for jobs with others around the world who are often willing to work longer hours for less money than American workers. And this is true not only for manufacturing jobs, which are routinely outsourced to other countries, but also for professional occupations such as medicine and accounting.

▶ **Innovative.** The economy depends on creativity in new products and services to generate consumer interest around the world. We are witnessing an unprecedented expansion of entrepreneurial businesses that have become the engine for new job growth.

▶ **Borderless.** Teams of workers within an organization need to understand the missions of other parts of the organization because they most likely will have to work together. U.S. companies also have partners throughout the world. In 2006, the French telecommunications company, Alcatel, acquired the American company, Lucent, to create one of the world's major suppliers of telecommunications equipment. Crossing borders has other implications. You might be an accountant and find yourself working with the public relations division of your company, or you might be a human resources manager who does training for a number of different divisions and in a number of different countries. You might even find yourself moved laterally—to a unit with a different function—as opposed to climbing the proverbial career ladder.

▶ **Customized.** More and more, consumers are demanding products and services tailored to their specific needs. For example, you surely have noticed the seemingly endless varieties of a single brand of shampoo or cereal crowding your grocer's shelves. Such market segmentation requires constant adaptation of ideas to identify new products and services as new customer demands emerge.

▶ **Fast.** When computers became popular, people rejoiced because they believed the computer would reduce their workloads. Actually, the reverse happened. Whereas secretaries and other support workers once performed many tasks for executives, now executives are designing their own PowerPoint presentations because, as one article put it, "It's more fun to work with a slide show than to write reports." For better or worse, "We want it now" is the cry in the workplace, with product and service delivery time cut to a minimum (the "just-in-time" policy). Being fast requires constant thinking outside the lines to identify new approaches to designing and delivering products.

▶ **Unstable.** Scandals within the highest ranks of major companies and constant mergers and acquisitions of companies have destabilized the workforce. Increases in oil prices have had a ripple effect through many sectors of the economy, and the practice of making "subprime" loans to unqualified home buyers has turned the housing market upside down. The global marketplace is constantly changing, so it's important to keep up-to-date on economic trends as they relate to your prospective major and career.

According to *Fast Company* magazine, the new economy has changed many of the rules about work. Leaders are now expected to teach and encourage others as well as head up their divisions. Careers frequently zigzag into other areas. People who can second-guess the marketplace are in demand. Change has become the norm. Workers are being urged to continue their learning, and companies are volunteering to play a critical role in the public welfare through sponsorship of worthy causes. With the lines between work and life blurring, workers need to find healthy balance in their lives. Bringing work home might be inevitable at times, but it shouldn't be the rule.

As you work, you'll be continually enhancing and expanding your skills and competencies. You can accomplish this on your own by taking evening courses or by attending conferences and workshops your employer sends you to. As you prepare over the next few years to begin your career, remember that:

▶ **You are, more or less, personally responsible for your career.** At one time organizations provided structured ladders that employees could climb to higher professional levels. In most cases such ladders have disappeared. Companies might assist you in assessing your own skills and might provide you information on available positions in the industry, but the ultimate task of creating a career path is yours.

▶ **To advance your career, you must accept the risks that accompany employment and plan for the future.** Organizations will continually restructure, merge, and either grow or downsize in response to economic conditions. As a result, positions might be cut. Because you can be unemployed unexpectedly, it will be wise to keep other career options in mind.

▶ **A college degree does not guarantee employment.** Of course, you'll be able to hunt for more opportunities that are rewarding, financially and otherwise, than if you did not have a degree. But just because you want to work for a certain organization doesn't mean there will always be a job for you there.

▶ **A commitment to lifelong learning will help keep you employable.** In college you have been learning a vital skill: how to learn. *Gradus,* the Latin root of *graduation,* means moving to a higher level of responsibility. Your learning has just begun when you receive your diploma.

Now the good news. Thousands of graduates find jobs every year. Some might have to work longer to get where they want to be, but persistence pays off. If you start now, you'll have time to build a portfolio of academic and *cocurricular experiences* that will begin to add substance to your career profile. Rudyard Kipling's verse from *Just So Stories* (1902) is an easy device for remembering how to navigate the fast economy for career success:

> *I keep six honest serving-men;*
> *(They taught me all I knew);*
> *Their names are What and Why and When*
> *And How and Where and Who.*

The knowledge to manage your career comes from you (why, who, how) and from an understanding of the career you wish to enter (what, where, when).

◀ **Networking is an important skill for opening the door to a future job.**

Aligning Your Sense of Purpose and Your Career

Why Why do you want to be a _____ ? Knowing your goals and values will help you pursue your career with passion and an understanding of what motivates you. When you speak with an interviewer, avoid clichés like "I'm a people person" or "I like to work with people." Sooner or later, most people have to work with people. And your interviewer has heard this much too often. Instead, be sure that you have crystallized your actual reasons for following your chosen career path. An interviewer will want to know why you are interested in the job, why it feels right for you at this time in your life, and whether you are committed to this career for the future.

  Who Network with people who can help you find out what you want to be. Right now, those people might be instructors in your major, an academic advisor, or someone at your campus career center. Later, network with others who can help you attain your goal. Someone will always know someone else for you to talk to.

  How Have the technical and communications skills required to work effectively. Become a computer whiz. Learn how to do PowerPoint presentations, build web pages, and create Excel spreadsheets. Take a speech course. Work on improving your writing. Even if you think your future job doesn't require these skills, you'll be more marketable with them.

  What Be aware of the opportunities an employer presents as well as threats such as *outsourcing* jobs. Clearly understand the employment requirements for the field you have chosen. Know what training you will need to remain in your chosen profession.

  Where Know the points of entry into the field. For example, you can obtain on-the-job experience through internships, co-ops, or part-time jobs.

  When Know how early you need to start looking. Find out whether certain professions hire at particular times of the year.

Connecting Your Major and Your Interests with Your Career

Some students are sure about their major when they enter college, but many others are at a loss. Either way, it's OK. At some point you should ask yourself, "Why am I in college?" Although it sounds like an easy question to answer, it's not. Many students would immediately respond, "So I can get an education for a good job or specific career." The problem is that most majors do not lead to a specific career path or job. You actually can enter most career paths from any number of academic majors. Marketing, a common undergraduate business major, is a field that recruits from a wide variety of majors including advertising, communications, and psychology. Sociology majors find jobs in law enforcement, teaching, and public service.

  Today English majors are designing web pages, philosophy majors are developing logic codes for operating systems, and history majors are sales representatives and business managers. You do not have to major in a science to gain admittance

Confessions of a College Student

Name: Mary Ann Williams

Age: 45

College: Midlands Technical College

Hometown: Columbia, South Carolina

Major: Nursing

Favorite books(s): *Of Mice and Men, Lonesome Dove*

Favorite college course: Intro to Psychology

Heroes: Celia Bowman, a coworker who returned to school to get her nursing degree.

Favorite way to relax: Reading at the beach

Your proudest moment or biggest accomplishment: Returning to college at the age of 45.

Favorite food: Dark chocolate

Career center confession: One of the assignments in my freshman seminar was to take a career assessment inventory at the career center. I'd never taken a career placement test before and didn't know what to expect. I was surprised to learn that I scored high in several career areas other than my chosen field. Although I plan to remain in my chosen field of nursing, it was helpful to know that I have other options should I decide to change my major. The career center and the programs it offers gave me the opportunity to learn something new and helpful about myself.

to medical school. Of course, you do have to take the required science and math courses, but medical schools seek applicants with diverse backgrounds. Only a few technical or professional fields, such as accounting, nursing, and engineering, are tied to specific majors.

Exploring your interests is the best way to choose an academic major. If you're still not sure, take the advice of Patrick Combs, author of *Major in Success*, who recommends that you major in a subject that you are really passionate about. Most advisors would agree.

Write • DISCUSS • Compare • Ask • BLOG • Answer • *Journal*

> Would you describe your major as a subject you're really passionate about? Why or why not? If your answer is no, why are you pursuing this particular major?

Chapter 1 suggested that you think very seriously about your purpose for being in college. Here are some additional questions to ask yourself as you continue thinking about why you're at this particular college or university.

▶ Am I here to find out who I am and to study a subject I am truly passionate about, regardless of whether it leads to a career?

▶ Am I here to engage in an academic program that provides an array of possibilities when I graduate?

▶ Am I here to prepare myself for a graduate program?

▶ Am I here to obtain specific training in a field I am committed to?

▶ Am I here to gain specific skills for a job I already have?

Some students will find they're not ready to select an academic major in the first year. You can use your first year, and even your second year, to explore your interests and see how they might connect to various academic programs. In the process of your exploration, you might later answer the question differently than you did during your first term.

You can major in almost anything. As this chapter emphasizes, it is how you integrate your classes with extracurricular engagement and work experience that will serve as a successful transition to your career. Try a major you think you'll like, and see what develops. But keep an open mind, and don't pin all your hopes on finding a career in that major alone.

Selecting a major and a career ultimately has to fit with your overall life goals, purposes, values, and beliefs.

Exploring Your Interests

John Holland, a psychologist at Johns Hopkins University, developed a number of tools and concepts that can help you organize the various dimensions of yourself so that you can identify potential career choices.

Holland separates people into six general categories based on differences in their interests, skills, values, and personality characteristics—in short, their preferred approaches to life:[1]

Realistic (R) These people describe themselves as concrete, down-to-earth, and practical doers. They exhibit competitive/assertive behavior and show interest in activities that require motor coordination, skill, and physical strength. They prefer situations involving action solutions rather than tasks involving verbal or interpersonal skills, and they like to take a concrete approach to problem solving rather than rely on abstract theory. They tend to be interested in scientific or mechanical areas rather than cultural and aesthetic fields.

Investigative (I) These people describe themselves as analytical, rational, and logical problem solvers. They value intellectual stimulation and intellectual achievement and prefer to think rather than to act, to organize and understand rather than to persuade. They usually have a strong interest in physical, biological, or social sciences. They are less apt to be people-oriented.

Artistic (A) These people describe themselves as creative, innovative, and independent. They value self-expression and relations with others through artistic expression

---

[1] Adapted from John L. Holland, *Self-Directed Search Manual* (Odessa, FL: Psychological Assessment Resources, 1985).

and are also emotionally expressive. They dislike structure, preferring tasks involving personal or physical skills. They resemble Investigative (I) people but are more interested in the cultural or the aesthetic than the scientific.

Social (S) These people describe themselves as kind, caring, helpful, and understanding of others. They value helping and making a contribution. They satisfy their needs in one-to-one or small-group interaction using strong speaking skills to teach, counsel, or advise. They are drawn to close interpersonal relationships and are less apt to engage in intellectual or extensive physical activity.

Enterprising (E) These people describe themselves as assertive, risk-taking, and persuasive. They value prestige, power, and status and are more inclined than other types to pursue these. They use verbal skills to supervise, lead, direct, and persuade rather than to support or guide. They are interested in people and in achieving organizational goals.

Conventional (C) These people describe themselves as neat, orderly, detail-oriented, and persistent. They value order, structure, prestige, and status and possess a high degree of self-control. They are not opposed to rules and regulations. They are skilled in organizing, planning, and scheduling and are interested in data and people.

Holland's system organizes career fields into the same six categories. Career fields are grouped according to what a particular career field requires of a person (skills and personality characteristics most commonly associated with success in those fields) and what rewards those fields provide (interests and values most commonly associated with satisfaction). Here are a few examples:

Realistic (R) Agricultural engineer, electrical contractor, industrial arts teacher, navy officer, fitness director, package engineer, electronics technician, computer graphics technician

Investigative (I) Urban planner, chemical engineer, bacteriologist, flight engineer, genealogist, laboratory technician, marine scientist, nuclear medical technologist, obstetrician, quality-control technician, computer programmer, environmentalist, physician, college professor

Artistic (A) Architect, film editor/director, actor, cartoonist, interior decorator, fashion model, graphic communications specialist, journalist, editor, orchestra leader, public relations specialist, sculptor, media specialist, librarian, reporter

Social (S) Nurse, teacher, social worker, genetic counselor, marriage counselor, rehabilitation counselor, school superintendent, geriatric specialist, insurance claims specialist, minister, travel agent, guidance counselor, convention planner

Enterprising (E) Banker, city manager, FBI agent, health administrator, judge, labor arbitrator, salary and wage administrator, insurance salesperson, sales engineer, lawyer, sales representative, marketing specialist

Conventional (C) Accountant, statistician, census enumerator, data processor, hospital administrator, insurance administrator, office manager, underwriter, auditor, personnel specialist, database manager, abstractor/indexer

Your career choices ultimately will involve a complex assessment of the factors that are most important to you. To display the relationship between career fields and the potential conflicts people face as they consider them, Holland's model is commonly presented in a hexagonal shape (Figure 4.1). The closer the types, the closer the relationships among the career fields; the farther apart the types, the more conflict among the career fields.

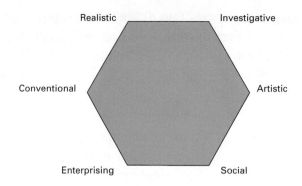

▶ **Figure 4.1**
Holland's Hexagonal Model of Career Fields

Holland's model can help you address the problem of career choice in two ways. First, you can begin to identify many career fields that are consistent with what you know about yourself. Once you've identified potential fields, you can use the career library at your college to get more information about those fields, such as daily activities for specific jobs, interests and abilities required, preparation required for entry, working conditions, salary and benefits, and employment outlook. Second, you can begin to identify the harmony or conflicts in your career choices. This will help you analyze the reasons for your career decisions and be more confident as you make choices.

Never feel you have to make a decision based on the results of only one assessment. Career choices are complex and involve many factors; furthermore, these decisions are reversible. Take time to talk your interests over with a career counselor. Another helpful approach is to "shadow" an individual in the occupation that interests you to obtain a better understanding of what the occupation entails in terms of skills, commitment, and opportunity.

Factors Affecting Career Choices

Some people have a definite self-image when they enter college, but most of us are still in the process of defining (or redefining) ourselves throughout life. We can look at ourselves in several useful ways with respect to possible careers:

▶ **Values.** Today, more than ever, knowing your core values (your most important beliefs) is important in shaping your career path. In a fast economy, having a strong rudder will help you steer through the turbulent times.

▶ **Interests.** Your interests can emerge from experiences and beliefs and will continue to develop and change throughout your life. You might be interested in writing for the college newspaper because you wrote for your high school paper. It's not unusual to enter Psych 101 with a great interest in psychology and realize halfway through the course that psychology is not what you imagined.

▶ **Skills.** The ability to do something well can usually be improved with practice.

▶ **Aptitudes.** Your inherent strengths, or aptitudes, are often part of your biological heritage or the result of early training. We each have aptitudes we can build on.

▶ **Personality.** Your personality makes you the person you are and can't be ignored when you make career decisions. The quiet, orderly, calm, detail-oriented person probably will make a different work choice than the aggressive, outgoing, argumentative person.

▶ **Life goals and work values.** All of us define success and satisfaction in our own way. The process is complex and very personal. Two factors influence our assessment of success and happiness: a) knowing that we are achieving the life goals we've set for ourselves, and b) finding that we gain satisfaction from our work. If your values conflict with the organizational values where you work, you might be in for trouble.

Your Career Planning Timetable

The process of making a career choice begins with

▶ Understanding your values and motivations

▶ Identifying your interests

▶ Linking your personality and learning styles to those interests

▶ Using this information to decide on an appropriate academic major

This is a process you will begin in your first year of college, and you will gradually complete it as you move closer to graduation. So don't worry about finishing this now. Also, not every student will follow this pattern. While this process is one way to begin investigating career possibilities, circumstances might force you to digress from this plan. Such circumstances might be a change of major or an unforeseen opportunity to intern. You will need to periodically reevaluate your plan to better suit your needs and any special characteristics of your major.

Creating a Plan

A good career plan should eventually include:

▶ Researching possible occupations that match your skills, interests, and academic major

▶ Building on your strengths and developing your weaker skills

▶ Preparing a marketing strategy that sells you as a valued member of a professional team

▶ Writing a convincing résumé and cover letter

Table 4.1 on page 56 provides a guide to what you should be doing during each year of college; if you are in a two-year associate degree program, you will have to do more during your second year than this table suggests.

Write • DISCUSS • Compare • Ask • BLOG • Answer • *Journal*

> What kinds of part-time jobs have you had, either for pay or as a volunteer? Which of your jobs was your favorite; which did you dislike? What do your experiences tell you about your preferences for work in the future?

Table 4.1   Your Career Itinerary

A. NO MATTER WHAT YEAR

▶ Get a job. Even a part-time job will develop your skills and might help you to make decisions about what you like—and what you don't—in a work environment. In any job, you can learn vital teamwork, communication, interpersonal, computer, and time-management skills.

▶ Register with your college's online job listing system to find listings for part- and full-time, internship, co-op, and seasonal employment.

▶ Find on-campus interviewing opportunities for internships in your first or second year and for full-time employment after graduation.

▶ Network with family, friends, instructors, friends of family, and acquaintances to find contacts in your field(s) of interest so that you can learn more about those areas.

▶ Volunteer! This can help you explore careers and get some experience in an area that interests you as you help others.

▶ Conduct occupational and industry research on your field or area of geographic interest. Look for other options within and beyond that field.

▶ Explore career options through informational interviews (interviewing to find out about a career) and job shadowing (observing someone at work—with their permission, of course).

▶ Prepare a draft of your résumé and have it critiqued by a career counselor and perhaps by a professional in your chosen field.

▶ Get involved in clubs and organizations; work toward leadership positions.

▶ Explore study possibilities in other countries to gain a global perspective and learn a foreign language.

▶ Attend career fairs to connect with employers for internships and other career-related opportunities as well as to develop a professional network.

B. FIRST YEAR OF COLLEGE

▶ Take the Holland Self-Directed Search or a similar interest inventory at your career center.

▶ Take a variety of classes to get exposure to various skill and knowledge areas.

▶ Attend your campus's annual career fair to see what is being offered.

▶ Talk to a career counselor about your skills, aptitudes, and interests. Find out what the career center offers.

Write • DISCUSS • Compare • Ask • BLOG • Answer • *Journal*

Have you explored your institution's career center? If so, what did you learn? If not, when in your college experience do you think going to the career center will be most important? Why?

C. SECOND YEAR OF COLLEGE

▶ Attend career fairs to learn more about employers who hire graduates in your major.

▶ Spend some time talking with your college advisor or career counselor to discuss your career plans.

D. THIRD YEAR OF COLLEGE

▶ Take an advanced computerized career assessment to discover further career options and to refine your career plans. Visit your career center.

▶ Take on a leadership role in a club or organization.

▶ Participate in mock interview activities to improve your interviewing skills.

Continued

> ▶ Attend workshops to learn more about résumé writing, looking for an internship, interviewing, and other job search skills.
>
> ▶ Explore the option of graduate school.
>
> ▶ Develop a top-ten list of employers of interest.

E. LAST YEAR OF COLLEGE

> ▶ Check on-campus interviewing opportunities on a daily basis, beginning in the fall term. Interview with organizations recruiting for your major.
>
> ▶ Research organizations of interest to you, interview with those coming to campus, and contact human resources professionals who represent organizations that won't be on campus. Find out whether you can interview.
>
> ▶ Attend career fairs to network with employers and set up interviewing opportunities.
>
> ▶ If you're thinking about graduate school, request applications early in the fall and send them out throughout the fall term.
>
> ▶ Target your geographic areas of interest by contacting local chambers of commerce and using local newspapers, phone books, and Internet resources.

Used by permission of Career Passport, Michigan State University.

Write • DISCUSS • Compare • Ask • BLOG • Answer • *Journal*

What kind of marketing strategy could you develop to sell yourself to a potential employer? Which of your characteristics or aptitudes would you emphasize?

You might proceed through these steps at a different pace than your friends, and that's OK. What you want is to develop your qualifications, make good choices, and take advantage of any opportunities on campus to learn more about the career search. Keep your goals in mind as you select courses and seek employment, but also keep an eye out for unique opportunities; the route you think you want to take might not be the best one for you ultimately.

Planning for Two-Year College Students

If you are a student attending a two-year college and you plan to transfer to a four-year college or university, your career planning timeline will be compressed. You might find that once you get to the four-year institution, you have less time to make adjustments in your course work and career opportunities. The major stumbling block is the fact that transfers often arrive on their new campus with enough credits to declare a major. At this point changing your major again can be costly because it will mean adding time, and therefore expense, before graduation.

Consider these early steps during your first three terms at your two-year college:

▶ Take a career-interest inventory.

▶ Begin focusing on the career paths that most interest you.

▶ Visit with a career counselor to develop a short-term strategy to test your career interests.

▶ Enroll in a career decision-making class.

▶ Job shadow a professional in the occupation(s) you wish to enter.

▶ Attend a local job fair (if possible) to learn about potential job opportunities.

During your last term at your two-year college, consider these options:

▶ Determine which academic majors best match your occupational interests.

▶ Investigate whether the college or university you will attend next has the majors you need, and learn about any prerequisites you will have to meet before you can enroll in your chosen major.

▶ If you still find you do not have a clear career focus by the time you transfer, meet again with the college's career advisor.

▶ Visit the campus you are transferring to prior to registration. Meet with both a career advisor and an academic advisor as soon as possible.

Starting Your Search for a Major and a Career

Some first-year students come to college with a strong sense of self-knowledge and a focus on a specific interest. Others have no idea what their interests might be and are in the process of sorting through their values, interests, and skills in an attempt to define themselves. Such self-definition is an ongoing experience that, for many of us, continues well beyond college. It helps to keep a journal of such thoughts because reviewing these early interests later in life might lead to long-forgotten career paths just when you need them.

As you start examining your aspirations and interests, keep in mind these simple do's and don'ts:

Do's

1. Do explore a number of career possibilities and academic majors.

2. Do get involved through volunteer work, study abroad, and student organizations—especially those linked to your major.

3. Do follow your passion. Learn what you love to do, and go for it.

Don'ts

1. Don't just focus on a major and blindly hope to get a career out of it. That's backwards.

2. Don't be motivated primarily by external stimuli, such as salary, prestige, and perks. All the money in the world won't make you happy if you hate what you're doing every day.

3. Don't select a major just because it seems cool.

4. Don't choose courses simply because your roommate or friend said they were easy. That's wasting your valuable time, not to mention your tuition.

Getting Experience

Now that you have a handle on your interests, it's time to test the waters and do some exploring. Your campus has a variety of activities and programs in which you can participate to confirm your interests and values as well as gain valuable skills. Here are some examples:

▶ **Volunteer/service learning.** Some instructors build service learning into their courses. *Service learning* allows you to apply academic theories and ideas to actual practice. Volunteering outside of class is also a valuable way to encounter different life situations and to gain work knowledge in areas such as teaching, health services, counseling, and tax preparation. A little time spent each week can provide immense personal and professional rewards.

▶ **Study abroad.** Spend a term taking courses in another country, and learn about a different culture at the same time. Learn to adapt to new traditions and a different pace of life. Some study-abroad programs also include options for both work and service learning experiences.

▶ **Internships and co-ops.** Many employers now expect these work experiences. They want to see that you have experience in the professional workplace and have gained an understanding of the skills and competencies necessary to succeed. Check with your academic department and your career center on the internships that are available in your major. Many majors offer academic credit for internships. And remember: With an internship on your résumé, you'll be a step ahead of students who ignore this valuable experience.

▶ **On-campus employment.** On-campus jobs might not provide as much income as off-campus jobs, but on-campus jobs give you a chance to practice good work habits. On-campus employment also brings you in contact with faculty and other academic professionals whom you can later consult as mentors or ask for references.

▶ **Student projects/competitions.** In many fields students engage in competitions based on what they have learned in the classroom. Civil engineers build concrete canoes, and marketing majors develop campaign strategies, for example. They might compete against teams from other colleges or universities. In the process they learn teamwork, communication, and applied problem-solving skills.

▶ **Research.** An excellent way to extend your academic learning is to work with a faculty member on a research project. Research extends your critical-thinking skills and provides insight on a subject beyond your books and class notes.

Skills Employers Look For

One of the many important outcomes of your college experience is the acquisition of a combination of knowledge and skills. Two types of skills are essential to employment and to life: content (mastery) skills and transferable skills.

Content Skills

Content skills, often referred to as cognitive, intellectual, or "hard" skills, are acquired as you gain mastery in your academic field and include writing proficiency, computer literacy, and foreign language skills. Computing knowledge and ability are now perceived as core skills of equal importance to reading, writing, and mathematics. In fact, employer expectations for computer knowledge and application continue to rise.

Content skills include specific types of information, facts, principles, and rules. For instance, perhaps you have knowledge of civil engineering related to dam construction, or you have extensive experience working with telescopes. Maybe your work in the library and study of library science has trained you in several library databases. Or you might know the most common clinical diagnoses in psychology. We often forget some of the preparation we have gained that augments our mastery of specific academic material, especially statistics, research methods, foreign language aptitude, and computer literacy. You can apply all of this specific knowledge to jobs in a particular field or occupation.

Certain types of employers expect extensive knowledge in your academic major before they will consider hiring you; for example, to get a job in accounting you must demonstrate knowledge of that field. For most college students, however, it's sufficient to have some fundamental knowledge; you will learn more on the job as you move from entry-level to more advanced positions.

Transferable Skills

Transferable skills are those that are general and apply to or transfer to a variety of settings. Examples of transferable skills include excellent public speaking, interpersonal understanding, seeing the big picture, grasping the application of a software program to a task, using available software to maintain home pages and transfer information, and providing leadership while working in a team environment. By category, these transferable skills are:

▶ Communication skills that demonstrate solid oral and listening abilities, in addition to a good foundation in the basic content skill of writing

▶ Presentation skills, including the ability to justify and persuade as well as to respond to questions about and serious critiques of your presentation material

▶ Leadership skills, or the ability to take charge or relinquish control according to the needs of the organization

▶ Team skills, or the ability to work collaboratively with different people while maintaining autonomous control over some assignments

▶ Interpersonal abilities that allow you to relate to others, inspire others to participate, or ease conflict between coworkers

▶ Personal traits, including showing initiative and motivation, being adaptable to change, having a work ethic, being reliable and honest, possessing integrity, knowing how to plan and organize multiple tasks, and being able to respond positively to customer concerns

▶ Critical thinking and problem solving, or the ability to identify problems and their solutions by integrating information from a variety of sources and effectively weighing alternatives

▶ A willingness to learn quickly and continuously

Transferable skills are valuable to many kinds of employers and professions. They give you flexibility in your career planning. You can gain transferable skills through a variety of activities. For example, volunteer work, study abroad, involvement in a student professional organization or club, and the pursuit of hobbies or interests can all build teamwork, leadership, interpersonal awareness, and effective communication abilities. Internships or career-related work are also valuable opportunities to practice these skills in the real world.

Key Competencies

While employers expect skills and related work experience from today's college graduates, they also have begun to focus on additional key competencies that are critical for success in the new knowledge economy.

▶ **Integrity.** Your employment will depend on being able to act in an ethical manner at work and in the community.

▶ **Innovation.** You should also be able to evaluate, synthesize, and create knowledge that will lead to new products and services. Employers seek individuals who are willing to take some risks and explore innovative and better ways to deliver products and services.

▶ **Initiative.** A great employee is able to recognize the need to take action, such as helping a team member, approaching a new client, or taking on assignments without being asked. Employers do not want employees who will wait passively for a supervisor to provide work assignments; they want people who will see what they have to do and do it.

▶ **Commitment.** Both employers and graduate schools look for a candidate's commitment to learning. They want you to express what you really love to study and are willing to learn on your own initiative. The best foundation for this competency is engagement in and excitement about an academic program.

Finding a Job While in College

Do you hope to get a job while you are in college? Before you do, be really honest with yourself: is this something you must do in order to pay for college or is something you want to do to maintain your lifestyle and acquire things you want? Or is it a combination of both? Most students work. Here are some things you should know about working in college.

Work can support the attainment of your college goals, provide you with the financial means to complete college, and help structure your time so that you are a much better time manager. It can help you meet people who will later serve as important references for graduate school and/or employment. Yet working too much can interfere with your college success, your ability to attend class, do homework, and participate in many other valuable college activities, such as group study, foreign study and travel, and group activities. Take some time to determine how much you need to work, and stay within reasonable limits.

Stated very simply, students who work more than fifteen hours a week have a lower chance of success in college. And students who work on campus are also more likely to graduate from college than students working off-campus.

On-Campus Jobs

If you want or need to work, explore on-campus opportunities as soon as (or even before) you arrive. If you have a *work-study award*, check with your student employment office for a listing of possible campus jobs for work-study students. Your career center can tell you how to access your college's online employment system. It probably handles all types of jobs. You might have to register, but that is easy, especially if you have a draft résumé to upload to a web-based form. College employment systems generally channel all jobs collected from faculty, advisors, and career counselors into one database, so it is convenient for you to identify the sorts of jobs you are looking for.

Many campuses offer an on-campus job fair early in the fall term. Even if you might not be interested at the time, a visit to the job fair will give you a great idea of the range and type of jobs available on campus. You will be pleasantly surprised to learn that there are more opportunities than washing dishes in the cafeteria. Job fairs usually include off-campus community employers as well, in part because your institution must spend some of the work-study funds it receives supporting off-campus work by students.

Off-Campus Jobs

The best places to start looking for off-campus jobs are your campus career center and/or your financial aid office. They might well have listings or websites with off-campus employment opportunities. Feel free to speak to a career counselor for suggestions.

▶ Learn the names of the major employers in your college's geographic area: manufacturers, service industries, resorts, etc. For example, some campuses are near UPS distribution centers, which are well known for favoring college students for lucrative part-time, union-scale wage jobs. Once you know who the major employers are, check them out, visit their websites, and learn the details.

▶ Every state in the country has a state agency to collect and disseminate information about available employment opportunities. Check out the relevant website and see if your state agency has an office in the community where you are attending college.

▶ Visit employment agencies, particularly those that seek part-time, temporary workers. This is a convenient, low-risk (for both you and the employer) way to "shop" for a job and to obtain flexible, short-term, low-commitment employment.

▶ Visit online job boards, and look at the classified ads in the local newspaper, in print or online. Also, don't forget the classifieds in the national press. Some national firms have jobs that can be done part-time in your area or even from your own living space.

▶ Check your campus student newspaper. Employers who favor hiring college students often advertise there.

▶ Most jobs are never posted. Employers find it easier to hire people recommended to them by current employees, friends, or the person vacating the position.

Faculty often hire students for their research labs based on performance in the classroom.

▶ Whom you know is important. Your friends who already work on campus or who have had an internship can be the best people to help you when you are ready to search for your job. In fact, nearly 50 percent of all student jobs are found through family and friends.

College students often view the choice of a career as a monumental and irreversible decision. But in its broadest sense, a career is the sum of the decisions you make over a lifetime. There is no right occupation just waiting to be discovered. Rather, there are many career choices you might find fulfilling and satisfying. The question to consider is: "What is the best choice for me now?"

Steps to Obtaining a Job and Beginning a Career

Building a Résumé

Before you finish college, you'll need a résumé—whether it's for a part-time job, for an internship or co-op position, or for a professor who agrees to write a letter of recommendation for you. Typically, there are two types of résumés: One is written in chronological format, and the other is organized by skills. Generally, choose the chronological résumé if you have related job experience, and choose the skills résumé if you can group skills from a number of jobs or projects under several meaningful categories. Try for one page, but if you have a number of outstanding things to say that won't fit on a single page, add a second page.

Writing a Cover Letter

When sending a cover letter, heed the following suggestions:

▶ Find out whom to write to. It's not the same in all fields. If you were seeking a marketing position at an advertising agency, you would write to the director of account services. If you were approaching General Motors regarding a position in the engineering department, you might write to either the director of human resources for the entire company or to a special human resources director in charge of engineering. Your academic advisor or career counselor can help you here. So can the Internet.

▶ Get the most recent name and address. Advisors or career counselors can guide you to references in your campus or career library. Never write, "To whom it may concern."

▶ Use proper format for date, address, and salutation.

Interviewing

The first year of college does not seem like a time to be concerned about interviews, certainly not for a job. However, students often find themselves in interview situations shortly after arriving on campus: vying for positions on the student residence governing board, finding an on-campus job, competing for a second-year scholarship, applying for a residence hall assistant position, choosing a summer job opportunity, and being selected for an internship or as a research assistant. Preparing for an interview begins the moment you arrive on campus because the interview is about you and how college has changed you. Students who haven't clarified their sense of purpose or who have only taken a little time to actually reflect on who they are and how they have changed can feel lost in an interview.

The purpose of the interview is to exchange information. The interviewer's goal is to evaluate you on your abilities and competencies in terms of what the organization is looking for. For you, the interview is an opportunity to learn more about the employer and whether the job would be a good fit with your aptitudes and preferences. Ideally, you will want to find a match between your interests and abilities, on the one hand, and the position or experience you are seeking, on the other.

Here are some important tips as you prepare for an interview:

▶ Check with a career counselor to see whether you can attend a mock interview. Usually designed for seniors as they prep for their on-campus interviews, mock interviews help students strategize and feel comfortable with an interview. Even if a mock interview session is not available to you, the career center can offer tips for you on handling an interview situation. Check your career center website for sample interview questions so that you can practice before an interview.

▶ Understand the nature of the *behavioral interview*. In a behavioral interview, the interviewer assumes that your past experiences are good predictors of your future abilities and performance. Interviewers want to hear stories about things that you have done that can help them assess your skills and behaviors. Often there is not a right or wrong answer. Answering a behavioral question can be hard. A method used

© White Packert/Getty Images

▶ **Be sure that your résumé is well-organized, clear, and free of any misspelled words or incorrect use of language.**

WIRED WINDOW

IN ADDITION TO CHECKING your résumé and references, potential employers will also use online resources to learn more about you. In a recent national survey of college employers, slightly more than 11% said that they review candidate profiles on social networking sites like MySpace and Facebook and more than 60% said that the information they find has at least some influence on their hiring decisions. Since a user outside of your Facebook network cannot see your profile, companies have asked their employees who are recent graduates or their college interns to research potential candidates. On profile pages, employers can find discrepancies between a candidate's résumé and his or her actual academic and work experience. Potential employers might even spot other kinds of information or see pictures that would make them think twice about hiring you. Keep in mind that most of the people making hiring decisions don't understand social networking websites the way you do—they are wary of sharing any personal information online. When they find that a potential candidate is comfortable sharing his or her party pictures, describing personal escapades that some might consider inappropriate, or allowing friends to post crude comments, they will seriously question the judgment of that applicant. Knowing this, what would you change about your Facebook and/or MySpace profile to make it more appropriate for viewing by potential employers?

Now that you know what employers are looking for when they search social networking websites to research potential employees, pretend you are an employer. Pick either Facebook or MySpace and search for your friends. What did you find? How many of your friends would you hire based solely on their profile page? How many would you not hire based on the information or pictures on their profile page? Why? What about your own profile? What would a potential employer find there, and how might he or she react?

---

at Michigan State University and other campuses to help students think through possible answers is the PARK method, which helps to focus on the most relevant aspects of your experience.

> P: The problem or situation (What happened?)
> A: The actions you took (What did you do?)
> R: The results or outcomes (What was the result of the actions you took?)
> K: The knowledge you gained and applied from the experience (What did you learn? How did you apply it?)

▶ Dress appropriately. Dress codes vary depending on the location of the interview and the type of interview (e.g., professional, student-focused). First impressions matter, so as a rule of thumb always dress neatly and conservatively. You can be somewhat casual for some types of employers, but it is better to dress too professionally (in a dress suit and polished shoes) than too informally.

Getting off to a Good Start in the Workplace

This textbook has been designed to assist you in achieving success in college. This chapter extends the lessons you've learned about college to making a successful transition into the workplace. You have learned that the workplace is dynamic, changing constantly, and is very different from the college classroom. Employers want their new college hires to start fast and adapt quickly to their work environments. The skills mentioned in this section support this rapid transition. The behaviors and competencies highlighted in this chapter are those employers focus on to identify new employees ready for promotion or for more challenging assignments. And some behaviors can quickly lead to disciplinary actions, even dismissal.

Your career can get off to a rocky start if you display inappropriate behavior or make poor ethical choices. Perhaps little or nothing happened when you missed a class or two. Your professor might have been willing to give you an extension on a paper or project deadline. Maybe you were pushed to get an assignment completed and so you copied material from several websites and dropped the material in your paper without proper citations or original thought. The consequences might have been minimal—maybe you received a B- rather than a B. You might have been involved in a team project although you were not very enthusiastic about the topic or the other members of the group. Your contribution was minimal, but you got a great grade because everyone else covered for you. Although these behaviors are occasionally overlooked in college, they will quickly get you in trouble at work. In the workplace, you might not get a second chance.

Employers, in response to a series of questions on disciplining new hires, listed the following most frequent behaviors leading to disciplinary actions:

Reason for disciplinary action	Occurrence: Fairly to Very Often (%)
Lack of commitment to work	52
Unethical behavior	46
Failure to follow instructions	41
Ineffective in teams	41
Missing assignments/deadlines	33

Source: CERI Research Brief 1-2007, *Moving Up or Moving Out of the Company?* Michigan State University.

Not all inappropriate behavior will result in a dismissal or firing. Most employers want new hires to succeed and might give young adults the opportunity to make corrections in their behaviors. When asked which behaviors could result in firing, employers indicated that repeatedly being late to work or missing assignment deadlines probably would result in termination. However, unethical behaviors, poor work attitude, and inappropriate use of technology would result in immediate dismissal. Technology use is a ticklish problem for many employers. The rapid increase in e-mail, text messaging, social networking websites like MySpace and Facebook, and blogs have challenged acceptable business communication. New hires need to be aware that the material they place in these environments is part of the public record and can be found by anyone. Companies are sensitive to their brand image and have little tolerance for comments that are derogatory to the company. A more serious problem for employers is the hacking done by new employees, not of external sites, but within the company's own system. Hacking might be the top ethical breach that companies face today. Avoid these behaviors if you do not want to be fired.

TOP SIX REASONS NEW COLLEGE HIRES ARE FIRED
Unethical behavior
Lack of motivation at work
Inappropriate use of technology
Failure to follow instructions
Being late for work
Missing assignment deadlines

Write • DISCUSS • Compare • Ask • BLOG • Answer • *Journal*

If you were an employer, what behaviors would cause you to fire an employee? Are any of those behaviors like some of those you see in college? What advice would you give to a new hire who was working for you?

Employers quickly identify the individuals they want to promote or move to more challenging assignments. When asked which behaviors or competencies grab their attention, two skill sets stood out. The most important attribute you can bring to the workplace is a willingness to take the initiative. Employers are looking for individuals who will accept responsibilities above and beyond the stated job, who will volunteer for additional activities, who will promote new ideas, and who will be self-starters (needing little stimuli from a supervisor).

Another important attribute is "self-management." Self-management encompasses skills that establish your accountability to the company. Skills include the ability to:

▶ Monitor and regulate work commitments (set priorities)

▶ Manage time

▶ Establish high performance levels (including completing work on time, understanding the quality indicators of work performance)

▶ Handle stress

▶ Provide and develop rapport with customers and coworkers

▶ Cope effectively with change

Four additional skill sets round out the characteristics cited by employers as key to promotion or job assignments:

▶ Personal attributes (dependable, friendly, patient, reliable, and respectful of diversity)

▶ Commitment to and passion for work

Leadership

 Ability to present ideas persuasively in written and oral forms (being good at show-and-tell)

These are all transferable skills from your college experience. Look back to the section on transferable skills and key competencies and you will see that every one of them is important in whichever path you choose after graduation.

Top Characteristics and Competencies that Employers Seek in Promotion/Job Assignments
Taking initiative
Self-management
Personal attributes
Commitment and passion for work
Leadership
Show-and-tell

WHERE TO GO FOR **HELP**

On Campus

Your College Website Search your campus career resources. Larger campuses might have specialized career service centers for specific professional schools and clusters of majors. Often student professional organizations, academic advisors, and departments provide relevant career information on their websites.

Career Center Almost every college campus has a career center where you can obtain free counseling and information on careers. A career professional will work with you to help you define your interests, interpret results of any assessment you complete, coach you on interview techniques, and critique your résumé. It's important to schedule an appointment. By the end of your first year you should be familiar with the career center—where it is located and the counselor responsible for your academic major or interests. You might also find opportunities for internships and practice here.

Academic Advising More and more advisors have been trained in what is known as developmental advising, or helping you see beyond individual classes and initiating a career search. Talking to your advisor is often the best place to start. If you have not declared a major—which is the case for many first-year students—your advisor might be able to help you with that decision as well.

Faculty On many campuses, faculty take an active role in helping students connect academic interests to careers. A faculty member can recommend specific courses that relate to a particular career. Faculty in professional curricula, such as business and other applied fields, often have direct contact with companies and serve as contacts for internships. If you have an interest in attending graduate school, faculty sponsorship is critical to admission. Developing a faculty mentor can open a number of important doors.

Library Some campuses have a separate library in the career center staffed by librarians whose job is to help you locate career-related information resources. Of course, all campuses have a main library containing a wealth of information on careers. The person who will be glad to help you is your reference librarian at the main desk. If you are a student on a large university campus, you might find additional libraries that are specific to certain professional schools and colleges within the university, such as business, education, law, medicine, music, and engineering; these are also excellent sources for career information.

Upperclass Students Ask whether they can help you navigate courses and find important resources. Upperclass students might also have practical experience gained from internships and volunteering. Since they have tested the waters, they can alert you to potential pitfalls or inform you of opportunities.

Student Organizations Professional student organizations that focus on specific career interests meet regularly throughout the year. Join them now. Not only will they put you in contact with upperclass students, but their programs often include employer representatives, helpful discussions on searching for internships or jobs, and exposure to current conditions in the workplace.

Online

Career Center Go to your career center's home page and check its resources, such as hot links to useful pages. For example: Occupational Information Network: http://online.onetcenter.org/ This federal government site has information on occupations, skill sets, and links to professional sites for selected occupations. This is a great place to get started thinking about your interests.

Mapping Your Future: http://www.mappingyourfuture.biz/ This comprehensive site provides support for those who are just starting to explore careers.

The Riley Guide: www.rileyguide.com. One of the best sites for interviewing, job search strategies, and other critical career tips.

My Institution's Resources

_____

_____

_____

_____

Engagement with Learning

In this chapter YOU WILL LEARN

▶ What *engagement* means and why it is important

▶ How engagement can improve the quality of your learning

▶ The value of learning teams

▶ How to establish an academic relationship with your instructors

▶ How to find a mentor in college

▶ What to do if things go wrong between your professor and you

How well will you be ENGAGED WITH LEARNING?

A?B?C?A?B?C?A?B?C?

Read the following questions and choose the answer that most fits you.

1 How do you think you will learn while you're in college?

(A) Professors will just tell me what I need to know. I'll listen and I'll learn.

(B) It will be a mix of reading and listening and maybe going to the library.

(C) For me to really learn, I'm going to have to really take an interest and really get involved in learning opportunities both in class and out of class.

2 How would you respond to an invitation to join a study group or learning team?

(A) I really don't like to do any kind of group work, so I'd say no.

(B) I might join a group if I thought everyone in the group were smarter than I and could tell me what I needed to know.

(C) The best way to learn is in a group. I would want to join so that I could share and compare my ideas with others.

3 What would you do if you thought you deserved a better grade on a test than you received from a professor?

(A) I'd call my parents and get them to call the professor.

(B) I would try to get the professor to change it. Maybe I could do some extra credit work.

(C) I would meet with the professor to discuss the grade to make sure that I understood my mistakes. If the professor wasn't willing to consider a grade change, I'd have to accept that. I wouldn't be rude or demanding.

4 How would you react in class if you really disagreed with a professor's opinion?

(A) I wouldn't say a word because it might affect my grade.

(B) I don't know what I would do; I hope I would have the courage to speak up.

(C) I would try to voice my opinion but do it calmly and respectfully.

5 Would you consider finding a mentor to help you while you're in college?

(A) No, I really don't think I need any help.

(B) I might consider this, but aren't mentors usually older people? I wouldn't know how to ask an older person to help me.

(C) Mentors can really make a positive difference, so I'm definitely going to try to identify someone, either a professor or a staff member, who would be willing to mentor me.

Review your responses. (A) responses indicate that you really haven't thought much about engagement in learning. (B) responses indicate that you have some understanding of the importance of engagement, but you'll need to learn more about it. (C) responses indicate that you understand how to be engaged in learning and why engagement is important. Whatever your responses, this chapter will help you learn more about this important topic and why it's so important to your college success.

Research reveals that students who become thoroughly *engaged* in their college experience stand a greater chance of success than those who do not. *Engagement* means active involvement in every aspect of college life. It means approaching every challenge with determination, whether those challenges are learning, activities, friendships, community work, or relationships with instructors.

According to the annual National Survey of Student Engagement, directed by George Kuh of Indiana University, students who engage more frequently in "deep" learning activities report greater educational and personal gains from college, participate in more enriching educational experiences, perceive their campus to be more supportive, and are more satisfied overall with college.[1] In college, you have almost unlimited opportunities to become engaged. One way to begin is to become acquainted with your college instructors, especially those who offer you the chance

[1] George Kuh, "Student Engagement: Pathways to Collegiate Success," *2004 Annual Report, National Survey of Student Engagement.* (Bloomington, Ind. University of Indiana, 2004).

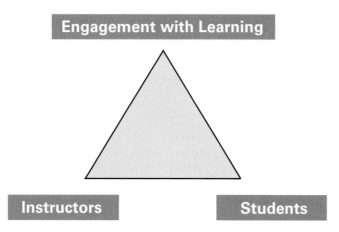

Engagement with Learning

Instructors   **Students**

▲ **Figure 5.1** When all three of these parts work in harmony, learning trends improve.

to learn *actively* rather than to be taught *passively*. Whenever your professor asks you a question in class, puts you in groups to solve a problem, requires you to make an oral presentation to the class, or does anything else that gives you and other students a voice in the learning process, you're more engaged in learning. As a result, while learning may not be any easier, it will be more productive. As Figure 5.1 indicates, learning depends on the engagement of both instructors and students.

Benefits of Engagement

Although you can acquire knowledge listening to a lecture, you may not be motivated to think about what that knowledge means. By being actively engaged in learning, you will learn not only the material in your notes and textbooks but also how to:

▶ Work with others.

▶ Improve your critical thinking, listening, writing, and speaking skills.

▶ Function independently and teach yourself.

▶ Manage your time.

▶ Gain sensitivity to cultural differences.

Engagement in learning requires preparation before and after every class, not just before exams. It might include researching in the library, making appointments to talk to faculty members, making outlines from your class notes, going to cultural events, working on a committee, asking someone to read something you've written to see whether it's clear, or having a serious discussion with students whose personal values differ from yours.

Write • DISCUSS • Compare • Ask • BLOG • Answer • *Journal*

Which of your current classes is the most engaging?
Least engaging? Why?

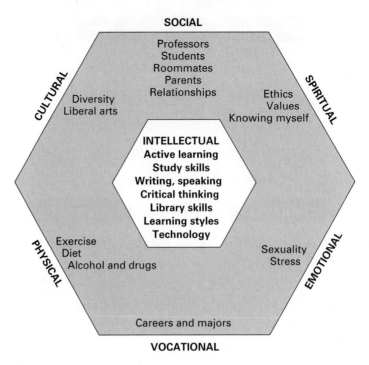

▲ **Figure 5.2** Aspects of student development.

This active approach to learning and living, in which you are connected to organizations, study with other students, sign up for classes that include community service, complete an internship, and so forth, has the potential to make you well-rounded in all aspects of life. The hexagon in Figure 5.2 depicts seven aspects of development, with intellectual development at its center. Optimal development depends on each area supporting every other area. With good active-learning skills, you likely will feel more comfortable socially, gain a greater appreciation for diversity and education, and be better able to clarify your major and future career. Staying physically active can reduce stress and keep your mind alert as you study. Developing a sense of values can help you choose your friends more carefully and decide how to manage your time.

The One-Minute Paper and Other Tips for Engagement

Another simple way to become engaged in learning is through a process called the *one-minute paper.* In a major study of teaching at Harvard University, one of many suggestions for improving learning was a simple feedback exercise.

At the end of each class, students were asked to write on what they thought was the main issue of that class and what their unanswered questions were for the next class. Using the one-minute paper helps your instructor to determine whether he or she provided a clear presentation and to use your unanswered questions for the next class. Even if your instructors don't require it, try writing a one-minute paper each day at the end of class. Use it to think about the main issues discussed that day, and

save it so that you will be prepared to ask good questions at the next class meeting. If you're in a study group or learning team, compare answers and questions; you may learn something!

Here are some additional things you can do to become engaged in learning:

▶ Ask friends which instructors employ active learning strategies before you choose a class.

▶ Even in a large class, sit as close to the front as you can to reduce distractions, and never hesitate to raise your hand if you don't understand something. Chances are your classmates don't understand it either.

▶ Put notes in your own words instead of just memorizing the book or the lecture.

▶ If you disagree with what your instructor says, politely challenge him or her. Good instructors will listen and may still disagree with you, but they will increase their respect for you when you show that you can think.

Collaborative Learning Teams

Because you'll be working with others after college, now is a good time to learn how to *collaborate*. Students who engage in learning through collaborative learning teams not only learn better but enjoy their learning experiences more.

Joseph Cuseo of Marymount College, an expert on collaborative learning, points to these advantages of taking a team approach to learning:

▶ Learners learn from one another as well as from the instructor.

▶ Collaborative learning is by its very nature active learning, and so it tends to increase learning through engagement.

WIRED WINDOW

ENGAGEMENT, as described in this chapter, means active involvement in every aspect of college life. Being involved in campus organizations and activities can enrich your college experience, expand your learning, and help you build strong connections with other students and faculty and staff. You may already be engaged in a virtual form of engagement through your use of Facebook and MySpace. Recent research suggests that students who are more engaged with their college friends on Facebook are more engaged on campus. While both of these social networking sites allow you through the groups feature to connect to other students

based on common interests, Facebook also allows students to connect to others in their courses through course applications. Through one such application, Courses 2.0, you can list the courses you are taking and automatically connect with other students taking the same course. That way, you can easily communicate with your new classmates about course assignments, due dates, and can even arrange real-world or virtual study groups. Additionally, you can learn about your classmates before the course even starts. Courses 2.0 is especially helpful for larger-section courses where it may be more difficult to connect with study partners.

▶ "Two heads are better than one." Collaboration can lead to more ideas, alternative approaches, new perspectives, and better solutions.

▶ If you're not comfortable speaking out in larger classes, you will tend to be more comfortable speaking in smaller groups, resulting in better communication and better ideas.

▶ You will develop stronger bonds with other students in the class, which may increase everyone's interest in attending.

▶ "Positive competition" happens when several teams are asked to solve the same problem—with the instructor clarifying that the purpose is for the good of all.

▶ Working in teams can help you develop leadership skills.

Maximizing Team Learning

Not all learning groups are equally effective. Sometimes teamwork is unsuccessful or fails to reach its potential because no thought was given to how the group was formed or how it should function. Use the following strategies to develop high-quality learning teams that maximize the power of peer collaboration:

1. Remember that learning teams are more than study groups. Effective student learning teams collaborate regularly by comparing notes, conducting library research, and reviewing for upcoming tests.

2. In forming teams, seek students who will contribute quality and diversity to the group. Resist the urge to include only your best friends. Look also for other students who are motivated, attend class regularly, are attentive, participate actively while in class, and complete assignments.

3. Keep the group small (four to six teammates). Smaller groups allow for more face-to-face interaction and eye contact and less opportunity for any one individual to shirk responsibility to the team.

4. Hold individual team members personally accountable for contributing to the learning of their teammates. One way to ensure accountability is to have each member come to group meetings with specific information or answers to share with teammates as well as questions to ask the group.

The Many Uses of Learning Teams

▶ **Note-taking teams.** Team up with other students immediately after class to share and compare notes so that your group will still have a chance to consult with the instructor about any missing or confusing information.

▶ **Reading teams.** After completing reading assignments, team with other students to compare your highlighting and margin notes. See whether all agree.

▶ **Library research teams.** This is an effective way to develop a support group for reducing "library anxiety" and for locating and sharing sources of information. This does not constitute cheating or plagiarizing as long as the final product you turn in represents your own work.

▶ **Team/instructor conferences.** Have your learning team visit the instructor during office hours to seek additional assistance as needed.

▶ **Team test results review.** After receiving test results, members of a learning team can review their individual tests together to help one another identify the sources of their mistakes and to review any tests that received high scores.

If you are a returning student, you and other returning students can form your own group to discuss the difference in your lives before college and now; or you can perhaps join a group of recent high school graduates to hear and provide a different point of view.

Using Learning Teams to Study Effectively in Math and Science

In his groundbreaking study of the factors that predict success in calculus, Uri Treisman of the University of Texas at Austin determined that the most effective strategy for success in calculus turned out to be active participation in a study group. It is now widely accepted that by working together as a team, students can significantly enhance each other's performance, especially in problem-solving courses like advanced math. Here are some things you can do to make learning teams a more effective way to study:

Compare Lecture Notes Look at the level of detail in each other's notes, and adopt the best of each other's styles. Discuss places in a problem where you got

© Digital Vision/Getty Images

lost. Talk about technical terms or symbols you didn't understand or couldn't decipher on the board and questions asked in class that you weren't able to hear.

Teach Each Other Split up the difficult topics and assign them to various members to prepare and present to team members. Remember that the best way to really learn something is to explain it to someone else.

Prepare for Tests Team members can divide the job of making a study outline. Each person brings his or her section. The members discuss and modify the outlines and a final version is created for all. Members can quiz one another, focusing on facts and specific pieces of information for an objective test and on how those pieces relate to one another for an essay exam. Members can then write practice questions for each other, or the group might create an entire sample exam and take it together under timed conditions. As you conclude each group study session, make a specific plan for the next meeting: "On Tuesday we'll use flash cards to be sure we understand the nervous system."

Provide Make-up Notes Of course, you should aim for perfect class attendance in all your courses. But if you absolutely have to miss a math or science class, your learning team is a source for notes and the assignment. If you do have to miss a class, it's important to get the notes from a study partner and catch up before the next class. Otherwise you have in effect missed two classes.

Ask the Right Questions Never criticize a question raised by a member of your learning team; respond cheerfully and express appreciation. Above all, come to the group meeting prepared, not with all the answers but knowing what specific questions you have.

Working with Your College Instructors

One of your greatest opportunities for learning in college will come from one-on-one interaction with a faculty member outside of class. Instructors are required to keep office hours; make an appointment to see them during that time. Don't feel as if you're bothering them. It's part of their job to be available for you.

Good instructors may be so enthusiastic about their fields of study that they talk quickly because they want to tell you the whole story. If you just can't keep up, raise your hand and politely ask them to slow down.

You can do a few simple things to improve relations between your instructors and you:

▶ Come to class regularly and be on time.

▶ Take advantage of office hours to see instructors when appropriate and get to know them.

▶ Realize that your instructors are not people to be avoided at all costs and that you will not be criticized by your peers if you're seen talking with them.

▶ Read the assigned material before class.

▶ Never talk or whisper while instructors are lecturing. They might interpret this as an uncaring or rude gesture.

▶ Don't hand your instructors phony excuses. They've been hearing these for years and can spot a false excuse a mile away. If you're sincere and give honest reasons for missing class or work, they're more likely to try and work around rules to help you.

If Things Go Wrong Between a Professor and You

What if you can't tolerate a particular instructor? Arrange a meeting to try to work things out. Getting to know the faculty member as a person can help you cope with the way he or she teaches the course. If that fails, check the class drop/add date, which usually falls at the end of the first week of classes. You may have to drop the course altogether and add a different one. If it's too late to add classes, you may still want to withdraw from the class by the official withdrawal date later in the term to avoid a penalty. See your academic advisor or counselor for help with this decision.

If you can't resolve the situation with the instructor and need to stay in the class, see the head of the department. If you are still dissatisfied, move up the administrative ladder until you get a definite answer. Never allow a bad instructor to sour you on college. If all else fails, realize that even the worst course will be over in a matter of weeks.

What if you're not satisfied with your grade? First, make an appointment to see the instructor and discuss the assignment. Your professor may give you a second chance because you took the time to ask for help. If you get a low grade on an exam, you might ask the instructor to review certain answers with you.

Never demand a grade change because this will most likely backfire.

Confessions of a College Student

Neil Corbett

Age: 23

University: McMurray University

Hometown: Ft. Worth, Texas

Major: English and Writing

Favorite book(s): *Hard-Boiled Wonderland and the End of the World* by Haruki Murakami and *On the Road* by Jack Kerouac

Favorite college course: Fiction Writing Workshop

The person who inspires me the most or whom I would most like to meet: J.D. Salinger or Bob Dylan

Heroes: Timothy Palmer, indie folk/pop star

Favorite way to relax: Read or play guitar

Your proudest moment or biggest accomplishment: When I finished writing my very first short story.

Favorite food: Bread

My engagement with learning confession:

I had several good relationships with professors. I went to a small university, which allowed the professors to work more closely with students. The instructors in my major and minor fields especially helped me with difficult class work. Of the few professors I didn't have particularly good relationships with (this was usually a result of my not caring for their teaching style) I generally just avoided taking their classes, or if it was unavoidable then I did my best and hoped for better luck next semester. The professors at McMurry all held scheduled office hours, during which time they were available to help students. I went regularly to have my professors look over drafts of papers or discuss writing topics. They were always helpful and willing to take a few minutes to work with me. If you're willing to take an interest in your education, then the professors are almost always willing to help you out.

Finding a Mentor

In his study of the aging process in men, the late Yale psychiatrist Daniel J. Levinson discovered several things about those who tended to be successful in life:

▶ They had developed a dream in adolescence, an idealized conception of what they wanted to become.

▶ They went on to find a mentor—an older, successful individual—who personified that dream.

▶ They also enjoyed friendships with a few other people who encouraged, nurtured, and supported them in their pursuit of their dream.

How do you find a mentor? Look for the person who takes a special interest in you, who encourages you to challenge yourself, who willingly listens to you when you have questions or problems, and who offers to meet with you to discuss your work. A mentor can be an academic advisor, instructor, department chair, older student, or anyone else who appears to offer interest, wisdom, and support. Most important, find a person you can trust, who will deal with you confidentially, and who is genuinely interested in your well-being while asking little or nothing in return.[2]

Write • DISCUSS • Compare • Ask • BLOG • Answer • *Journal*

A mentor is a person who is now, in some respects, what you hope to be in the future. What mentors have you had? What specific qualities have you tried to emulate? What are you seeking in a college mentor? If you have a mentor now, what might you do to make more use of this person? If you don't have a mentor, how might you find one during your first year of college?

▶ WHERE TO GO FOR **HELP**

On Campus

Learning (Assistance/Support) Center Almost every campus has one or more of these.

Sometimes they provide help for students in all subjects at all levels; sometimes they are specific to one discipline, such as math or English. The staff will know many, if not all, of your instructors and can provide good advice in using active-learning strategies.

These centers typically retain outstanding undergraduate students who serve as tutors. From their experience, they can teach you how to make active learning easier and more fun. Above all, remember: Learning centers are not just for students with serious academic problems—they are for all students who want to improve their learning skills.

Counseling Center Maybe your relationships with friends, partners, professors, and courses are putting you under excessive stress. This is a fairly common situation among new college students. There's help right on campus at the counseling center, which provides free and confidential support for students.

You can get insight into the sources of your stress and learn some new healthy coping mechanisms. You already have paid for such services in your basic tuition and fees. And seeking a counselor simply means that, as a new student with concerns, you are quite normal.

Faculty Members Probably at least one of your instructors has struck you as approachable and sympathetic. Make an appointment to see this person and share your concerns. He or she may have had similar concerns when beginning college. Certainly the authors of this book did.

Academic Advisor or Counselor Make a special effort to meet your advisor or counselor, especially if you're having problems with any of your courses or if circumstances are keeping you from earning higher grades.

And remember, if you don't feel comfortable with your advisor, you have the right to change advisors. Just ask someone in your departmental office or campus advising center.

[2] D. J. Levinson et al., *The Seasons of a Man's Life* (New York: Ballantine, 1978).

Thinking Critically

In this chapter YOU WILL LEARN

▶ Why there are no "right" and "wrong" answers to many important questions

▶ Four aspects of critical thinking

▶ How critical arguments differ from emotional arguments

▶ How college encourages critical thinking

▶ Why critical thinking is the basis for a liberal education

▶ The importance of critical thinking beyond college

© Andrew Douglas/Masterfile

How Do Your CRITICAL THINKING SKILLS Measure Up?

A?B?C?A?B?C?A?B?C?

Read the following questions and choose the answer that most fits you.

1 **When you hear other people arguing strongly for a particular idea, how do you decide whether the argument is valid?**

A I want to know something about them, such as what church they attend or whether they're members of my favorite political party.

B I can tell by the way they look and their tone of voice.

C I really listen to them carefully, then I seek other evidence to support or reject their arguments.

2 **When you make a decision, do you let your emotions get in the way?**

A Sometimes I am able to repress my anger or disappointment and think logically, but other times, my emotions just take over.

B Aren't your emotions what should guide your actions? I always think with my heart.

C I am pretty successful at thinking with my head first and can separate out my emotions.

3 **When you find a person irritating, can you still listen to what he or she has to say?**

A It depends on how irritating the person is—sometimes I can, but other times people can be so annoying that I just can't listen.

B Never—you just can't reason or talk with people like that.

C I think everyone deserves to be heard and can add to a discussion in some way.

4 **Do textbooks give you all the answers you need?**

A It depends on the course; some books have the answers to everything you need to know.

B Of course they do! Why else would the book be written, sold, and required for me to read?

C I don't think so. If I'm looking for answers, I like to read lots of different sources to learn other points of view, including the textbook.

5 **Do you believe that critical thinking is a desirable skill for prospective employers?**

A Some jobs require more critical thinking than others; some jobs might just need a robot to do the work.

B No—as long as you can get the work done for them, why does it matter?

C I think so. An employer will see that you are willing to problem solve and come up with alternatives that no one else might have considered.

Review your responses. **A** responses indicate that you have some understanding about critical thinking. But you'll need more practice applying thinking skills. **B** responses indicate that you haven't really thought much about what it means to think critically. **C** responses indicate that you have a good conceptual understanding of what critical thinking is all about. Whatever your responses, this chapter will help you learn more about this important skill, which you will use in college and beyond.

College has been described as "an investment in your future." That idea suggests that college not only can prepare you for a career but also can broaden your horizons in other ways. From history classes, you may develop an interest in the French Revolution and other aspects of French culture. From music appreciation, you may become a regular concertgoer. A literature course can help you discover the authors you will be reading long after you've said goodbye to campus. From other courses, you can develop interests in world travel, native crafts, or theater.

As you have new experiences and explore new ideas, you will begin to realize that life is full of ambiguities and that there may be many good answers to a single question. You will learn to question, to probe, and to demand evidence in support of claims. In short, you will learn to think critically.

College Helps You Develop Critical Thinking Skills

Theodora Kalikow, president of the University of Maine at Farmington, describes what characteristics college students should have in order to become good critical thinkers:

▶ A flexible mind, able to move rapidly in new directions.

▶ The ability to analyze a problem.

▶ The ability to imagine solutions, weigh them by rational *criteria* or standards, and commit to one of them.

▶ An understanding of the investigative approaches of various disciplines in order to acquire the ability to become one's own best lifelong teacher.

▶ A skepticism of superficial arguments and easy solutions and a distrust of simplistic analysis.

▶ A tolerance for ambiguity and complexity.

▶ An ability to imagine and share the perceptions of different individuals, cultures, and time periods.

▶ An appreciation of the community, of one's place in it, and of the need to contribute to society through public and private service.[1]

When you earn your college degree and land a job, chances are your employer is going to be more interested in how well you think than in how many bits of information you can memorize. Employers hiring college graduates often say they want an individual who can find information, analyze it, organize it, draw conclusions from it, and present it convincingly to others. These skills are the basic ingredients of critical thinking. Good critical thinkers can also:

▶ Manage and interpret information in a reliable way.

▶ Examine existing ideas and develop new ones.

▶ Pose logical arguments that further the absorption of knowledge. In the context of critical thinking, the term *argument* refers not to an emotional confrontation but to reasoning and information brought together in logical support of some idea.

▶ Recognize reliable evidence and form well-reasoned conclusions.

Critical thinking is a process of choosing alternatives, weighing them, and considering what they suggest. It involves understanding why some people believe one thing rather than another—whether you agree with those reasons or not. Critical thinking is learning to ask pertinent questions and testing your assumptions against hard evidence.

---

[1] Theodora J. Kalikow, "Misconceptions about the Word 'Liberal' in Liberal Arts Education," *Higher Education and National Affairs* (1998).

Walking Through the Process

When thinking about whether to support a logical argument, a good critical thinker considers questions like the following:

▶ Is the information given in support of the argument true?

▶ Does the information really support the conclusion?

▶ Do you need to withhold judgment until better evidence is available?

▶ Is the argument really based on good reasoning, or does it appeal mainly to your emotions?

▶ Based on the available evidence, are other conclusions equally likely (or even more likely)? Is there more than one right or possible answer?

▶ What more needs to be done to reach a good conclusion?

Good critical thinking also involves thinking creatively about what assumptions may have been left out or what alternative conclusions may not have been considered. When communicating an argument or idea to others, a good critical thinker knows how to organize it in an understandable, convincing way in speech or in writing.

Write • DISCUSS • Compare • Ask • ʙʟᴏɢ • Answer • *Journal*

> Have you ever fallen victim to a false claim for a product? Have
> you ever purchased something that turned out to be different
> from what you had been led to believe?

Critical Thinking and a Liberal Education

Most colleges and universities in the United States believe it's important to offer students what they call a "liberal" education. A liberal education has nothing to do with politics but is defined as education that "enlarges and disciplines the mind" through exposure to different ideas and fields of study. Learning to think critically is at the core of a liberal education. Critical thinkers learn to investigate all sides of a question and all possible solutions to a problem before reaching a conclusion or planning a course of action. They work hard to understand why some people believe one thing rather than another—whether or not they agree with them.

Write • DISCUSS • Compare • Ask • ʙʟᴏɢ • Answer • *Journal*

> What are the "liberal arts" (general education) courses you are
> taking this term? Explore how one (or more) of them is helping
> you to see the world in a new way.

Four Aspects of Critical Thinking

Critical thinking cannot be learned overnight. As interpreted by William T. Daly, professor of political science at The Richard Stockton College of New Jersey, the critical thinking process can be divided into four basic steps. Practicing these basic ideas can help you become a more effective critical thinker.

1. Abstract Thinking: Using Details to Discover Some Bigger Idea

From large numbers of facts, seek the fundamental ideas or *principles* behind the facts. What are the key ideas? Even fields like medicine, which involve countless facts, are grounded in general ideas such as the principles of circulation or the basic mechanisms of cell division.

Ask yourself what larger concepts the details suggest. For example, you may read an article that describes how many people are using the Internet now, how much consumer information it provides, what kinds of goods you can buy cheaply over the Internet, and

also how many low-income families are still without computers. By thinking carefully about these facts, you might arrive at several different important generalizations.

One generalization is that as the Internet becomes more important for shopping, the lack of computers in low-income households puts poor families at an even greater disadvantage. Or your general idea might be that because the Internet is becoming important for selling things, companies will probably find a way to put a computer in every home.

WIRED WINDOW

WEB LOGS, OR BLOGS, ALLOW ANYONE, even those with limited web-publishing experience, to post online journals that look professional. Blogs emerged in 2003 and their popularity has only increased, with Internet users creating over 100,000 new blogs every day. Because there are so many blogs, they cover just about any topic you can think of—from politics to purchasing, movies to money, sex to Silicone Valley. If you want to know a blogger's opinion about anything, you can find it in the blogosphere. Because there are so many blogs, opinions about an issue can range widely among bloggers, with some supporting a certain viewpoint, some being against it, and many others being somewhere in between. To sharpen your critical thinking skills, Google a current event that you find interesting. Next, search for blogs with commentary on the topic. (Hint: Search for the topic keywords plus the word "blog.") Find two blogs with different viewpoints on the same topic. To help you, review the four aspects of critical thinking and answer the following questions: What is each blogger's viewpoint? Do the people who leave comments generally agree or disagree with the blogger's point of view? Why does the blogger hold that point of view? Is there any evidence on the blog that supports the blogger's view? Do you have an opinion on the topic? Which blogger do you most agree with? Why?

2. Creative Thinking: Seeking Connections, Finding New Possibilities, Rejecting Nothing

Use the general idea you have found to consider what further ideas it suggests. The important thing at this stage is not to reject any of your ideas. Write them all down. You'll narrow this list in the next step.

The creative phase of thinking can lead in many directions. It might involve searching for ways to make the Internet more available to low-income households. Or it can involve searching out more detailed information on how much interest big companies really have in marketing various goods to low-income families. In essence, the creative thinking stage involves extending the general idea—finding new ways to apply it or identifying other ideas it might suggest.

3. Systematic Thinking: Organizing the Possibilities, Tossing Out the Rubbish

Systematic thinking involves looking at the outcome of the second phase in a more demanding, critical way. This is where you narrow that list from step 2. If you are looking for solutions to a problem, which ones really seem most promising after you have conducted an exhaustive search? Do some answers conflict with others? Which ones can be achieved? If you have found new evidence to refine or further test your generalization, what does that new evidence show? Does your original generalization still hold up? Does it need to be modified? What further conclusions do good reasoning and evidence support? Which notions should be abandoned?

4. Precise Communication: Being Prepared to Present Your Ideas Convincingly to Others

Intelligent conclusions aren't very useful if you cannot share them with others. Consider what your audience will need to know to follow your reasoning and be persuaded. Remember to have facts in hand as you attempt to convince others of the truth of your argument. Don't be defensive; instead, just be logical.

How College Encourages Critical Thinking

Many college students believe that their professors have all the answers. Unfortunately, most important questions do not have simple answers, and you will discover numerous ways to look at important issues. In any event, you must be willing to challenge assumptions and conclusions, even those presented by experts.

To challenge how you think, a good college professor will insist that how you solve a problem is as important as the solution and might even ask you to describe that problem-solving process.

Because critical thinking depends on discovering and testing connections between ideas, your instructor may ask open-ended questions that have no clear-cut answers, questions of why, how, or what if. For example: "In these essays we

Confessions of a College Student

Taylor McFadden

Age: 18

College: Purchase College

Hometown: West Nyack, New York

Major: Dance

Favorite book(s): *The DaVinci Code*

Favorite college course: Culture and Society in the West

The person who inspires me the most or whom I would most like to meet: Condoleezza Rice

Heroes: My parents

Favorite way to relax: A dance class or swimming

Your proudest moment or biggest accomplishment: Being accepted into a ballet company after many years of training.

Favorite food: Pretty much anything except fast food.

Critical thinking confession: Using critical thinking, I can evaluate the pros and cons of each topic logically. As a dancer, I tend to be a perfectionist, yet my critical thinking skills help me to understand that nobody is perfect. Faced with making a decision, I now can sort my priorities and come up with a better decision. Unfortunately, image is very important in our society and is fueled by advertising depicting people deemed by society as "perfect." I am grateful that critical thinking helps me look beyond those stereotypes and appreciate who I am.

have two conflicting ideas about whether bilingual education is effective in helping children learn English. What now?" Your instructor may ask you to break a larger question into smaller ones: "Let's take the first point. What evidence does the author offer for his idea that language immersion programs get better results?" She or he may insist that more than one valid point of view exists: "So for some types of students, you agree that bilingual education might be best? What other types of students should we consider?"

Your instructor may require you to explain clearly your reason for rejecting a point. "You think this essay is flawed. Well, what are your reasons?" Or he or she may challenge the authority of experts: "Dr. Fleming's theory sounds impressive. But here are some facts he doesn't account for . . ." You may discover that often your instructor reinforces the legitimacy of your personal views and experiences: "So something like this happened to you once, and you felt exactly the same way. Can you tell us why?" And you also will discover that you can change your mind.

In discovering that answers are seldom entirely wrong or right but more often somewhere in between, it is natural for new college students to find this mode of critical thinking difficult. Yet the questions that lack simple answers usually are the ones most worthy of study.

If you hang on to these rules, we can't promise that your classes will be any easier, but we can promise they certainly will be more interesting, for now you will know how to use logic to figure things out instead of depending purely on how you feel or what you've heard about something.

Write • DISCUSS • Compare • Ask • BLOG • Answer • *Journal*

Which of the courses you are currently taking encourage you to think critically, and which seem to depend more on right and wrong answers? In which courses do you feel you're learning the most?

A good class becomes a critical thinking experience. As you listen to the instructor, try to predict where the lecture is heading and why. When other students raise issues, ask yourself whether they have enough information to justify what they have said. And when you raise *your* hand to participate, remember that asking a sensible question may be more important than trying to find the elusive "right" answer.

The best way to learn, practice, and develop critical thinking skills is to take demanding college courses that provide lots of opportunities to think out loud, discuss and interact in class, and especially to do research and write, write, write. Take courses that use essay examinations as opposed to relying on multiple choice, true/false, or short answers. These last three types of exams are much less likely to develop your critical thinking skills.

Critically Evaluating Information on the Internet

Anyone can put anything on the Internet. An academic researcher found a movie review on the Internet, printed it, and discussed it in his seminar, only to realize later that it was written by an adoring fan, not an authoritative critic.

It is often difficult to tell where something on the Internet came from, how it got there, or who wrote it. In other words, the lack of a *citation*—information about the source—makes it difficult to judge the credibility of the information. So the first thing to do is to look for a citation. Then, using the citation, do a search for the original source and evaluate its authenticity. If there is no citation, chances are you should avoid the site. Ask yourself other questions, too.

Is It Credible? Is it the original source? Is it quoted out of context—that is, lifted in part from a more complete original source? Plagiarized? Altered—intentionally or unintentionally—from the original? Has the material been reviewed by experts?

Who Is the Author? What can you find out about her or him? Is she or he qualified to write this article? If you can't find information on the author, think twice before using the information. Beware of sites that have no date on a document, make sweeping generalizations, and use information that is biased and does not acknowledge opposing views.

Does It Reflect Mainstream Opinions? Whether you're looking for a fact, an opinion, or some advice, it is a good idea to find at least three sources that agree. If the sources do not agree, do further research to find out the range of opinion or disagreement before you draw your conclusions. If a site is sponsored by an *advocacy group*, be aware of the group's agenda or cause; that will affect the reliability of the information.[2]

How and Where to Check

Check online directory sources for affiliations and bibliographical information.

Look for other works by the author. Read a few of them. How accurate and unbiased do they sound?

Most print matter (books, articles, and so forth) has been reviewed (vetted) by an editorial board. Frequently it's difficult to confirm that the same is true for information from an Internet source, with some exceptions. If you are searching through a database, such as the Human Genome Database, the Civil War Database, or ERIC, the Education Resources Information Center, it is highly likely that sources from these collections have been reviewed by the database administrators.

Of course, you can use search engines, too; but you should compare the information you find through them with information from print sources or at least two other vetted electronic databases.

Ten Cs for Evaluating Internet Sources

The library at the University of Wisconsin at Eau Claire offers these additional suggestions for checking Internet sources:

Content What is the intent of the content? Are the title and author identified? Is the content "juried" or certified as accurate by other experts? Is the content "popular" or "scholarly," satiric or serious? What is the date of the document or article? Is the edition current? Do you have the latest version? (Is this important?) How do you know?

Credibility Is the author identifiable and reliable? Is the content credible? Authoritative? Should it be? What is the purpose of the information? Is it serious, satiric, humorous? Is the URL extension .edu, .com, .gov, or .org? What does this tell you about the publisher?

Critical Thinking How can you apply critical thinking skills, including previous knowledge and experience, to evaluate Internet resources? Can you identify the author, publisher, edition, and so on as you would with a traditionally published resource? What criteria do you use to evaluate Internet resources?

Copyright Even if the copyright notice does not appear prominently, someone wrote, or is responsible for, the creation of a document, graphic, sound, or image, and the material falls under copyright conventions. "Fair use" exemption from copyright

---

[2] Excerpt from VirtualSalt.com, http://www.virtualsalt.com. Reprinted by permission.

restriction applies to short, cited excerpts, often used as an example in commentary or research. Materials are in the public domain if this is explicitly stated. Internet users, as users of print media, must respect copyright.

Citation Internet resources should be cited to identify sources used, both to give credit to the author and to provide the reader with avenues for further research. Standard style manuals (print and online) provide examples of how to cite Internet documents, although these standards are not uniform.

Continuity Will the Internet site be maintained and updated? Is it now and will it continue to be free? Can you rely on this source over time to provide up-to-date information? Some good .edu (education) sites have become .com (commercial) sites. Other sites offer partial use for free but charge fees for continued or in-depth use.

Censorship Has your discussion list been "evaluated"? Messages posted to a moderated list are reviewed by a moderator before they are distributed to the entire list. Does your search engine or index look for all words or are some words excluded? Is this censorship? Does your institution, based on its mission, parent organization, or space limitations, apply some restrictions to Internet use? Consider censorship and privacy issues when using the Internet.

Comparability Does the Internet resource have an identified comparable print or CD data set or source? Does the Internet site contain comparable and complete information? (For example, some newspapers have partial rather than full text information on the Internet.) Do you need to compare data or statistics over time? Can you identify sources for comparable earlier or later data? Comparability of data may or may not be important, depending on your project.

Context What is the *context* (frame of reference) for your research? Can you find commentary, opinion, narrative, statistics, and so forth? Are you looking for current or historical information? Definitions? Research studies or articles? How does Internet information fit in the overall information context of your subject? Before you start searching, define the research context and research needs, and decide which sources might be used to successfully fill information needs without data overload.

▶ WHERE TO GO FOR HELP

On Campus

Logic Courses Check out your philosophy department's course in "Introduction to Logic." This may be the single best course designed to teach you critical thinking skills. Virtually every college offers such a course.

Argument Courses and Critical Thinking Courses These are usually offered in the English department. They will help you develop the ability to formulate logical arguments and avoid such pitfalls as "logical fallacies."

Debating Skills Some of the very best critical thinkers are those who developed debating skills during college. Go to either your student activities office or your department of speech/drama and find out whether your campus has a debate club, society, or team. Debating can be fun and chances are you would meet some interesting student thinkers.

Online

Check the following website for a critical review of a book titled The Encyclopedia of Stupidity: **http://arts .independent.co.uk/books/reviews/article112328.ece.**

Listening, Note-Taking, and Participating

In this chapter YOU WILL LEARN

▶ How to assess your note-taking skills and how to improve them

▶ Why it's important to review your notes soon after class

▶ How your five senses can assist in learning and remembering

▶ How to prepare before class

▶ How to listen critically and take good notes in class

▶ Why you should speak up in class

▶ How to review class and textbook materials after class

© AFP/Getty Images

Jeanne I. Higbee of the University of Minnesota-Twin Cities contributed her valuable and considerable expertise to the writing of this chapter.

How Do You LISTEN, TAKE NOTES, and Become ENGAGED in Class?

A?B?C?A?B?C?A?B?C?

Read the following questions and choose the answer that most fits you.

1   How would you prepare for a class beforehand?

(A) I sometimes glance at the syllabus to see what we're covering, but that's usually all I do.

(B) I read the assigned materials and go over my notes from the previous class; it helps me get focused for the class.

(C) I eat my breakfast or lunch and show up for class.

2   If you arrive at class early, how do you spend your time there?

(A) Depending on where my seat is, I'll either chat with some friends if they're nearby or take a peek at the chapter I should have read.

(B) I try to go over my notes before class starts so that I refresh my memory and get geared up for the class.

(C) I text message some friends to see what we'll be doing after classes.

3   If the instructor puts an outline on the board or overhead projector, how do you take notes?

(A) I listen the first time and then try to write everything down afterwards, but I usually have trouble remembering, and I then miss what the instructor talks about next.

(B) I write down the main points and stop to listen, then put what the instructor said in my own words.

(C) I think I have a photographic memory, so I don't need to write anything down.

4   If you realized that you missed something important in your notes, what would you do?

(A) Maybe I'd ask my friend in the class, if I remembered before the exam.

(B) I make sure I have someone reliable in my class whom I can exchange notes with in case I miss something. If we both missed it, I'd go to my instructor during office hours to get what I missed.

(C) I don't usually realize I missed something until late the night before an exam, so there wouldn't be anything I could do about it.

5   If you do not understand something in class, what do you do?

(A) In smaller classes, I'd probably ask a question, but never in a large lecture—that's too embarrassing.

(B) I would ask a question if there's something I don't understand, or wait until after class to ask the instructor for clarification.

(C) I'd just assume it's not important.

Review your responses. (A) responses indicate that you have some idea of how to listen, take notes, and become engaged in the classroom, but in order to do your best, you'll need to improve. (B) responses indicate that you have a good idea of important learning strategies to use in the classroom (C) responses indicate that you need to develop a better understanding of what it takes to do well in college classes. Wherever you are in your current understanding, this chapter will help you learn more about the basics of success in the classroom.

In virtually every college class you take, you'll need to master three skills to earn high grades: listening, note-taking, and participating. Taking an active role in your classes—asking questions, contributing to discussions, and providing answers—will help you listen better and take more meaningful notes. That in turn will enhance your ability to learn, understand abstract ideas, find new possibilities, organize those ideas, and recall the material once the class is over.

These skills are critical to your academic success because your college instructors are likely to introduce new material in class that your textbooks don't cover, and chances are that much of this material will resurface on quizzes and exams.

Here are some helpful tips for assuring that you will retain what is important from class:

1. Instead of chatting with friends before class begins, review your study notes from the previous class.

2. If you would like to record a lecture, be sure to ask the instructor's permission first. But keep in mind that it will be difficult to make a high-quality recording in an environment with so much extraneous noise. And even though you're recording, take notes. Also consider asking the instructor to speak more slowly or to repeat key points. You also may find it helpful to meet with a study group to compare notes on the lecture content.

3. Choose the note-taking system that works for you. If a formal outline works for you, fine. If it doesn't, consider other suggestions provided in this chapter for organizing your notes so you can go back to them later and understand them.

4. Be aware that what the instructor says in class may not always be in the textbook, and vice versa. And the instructor often believes what he or she said in class is more important than what is in the textbook; therefore, you are more likely to see lecture rather than textbook material on a test.

5. Since writing down everything the instructor says is probably not possible and later you might not be sure what's important, ask questions in class. This will ensure that you more clearly understand your notes. Reviewing your notes with a tutor or someone from your campus learning center or comparing your notes with a friend can also help you get an idea of the most important points.

6. If something is not clear, ask the instructor either in class or after class. Your friends may not have gotten it either or may have misunderstood the point the instructor was making. Remember that the instructor is always the best source.

7. And be sure to speak up! When you have a question to ask or a comment to share, don't let embarrassment or shyness stop you. You will be more likely to remember what happens in class if you are an active participant.

Write • DISCUSS • Compare • Ask • BLOG • Answer • *Journal*

> Think about how well you listen in class. How do time of day, temperature of the room, size of the class, and personality of the instructor affect your ability to listen? What about you—what personal behaviors increase or reduce your level of attentiveness in the classroom?

Understanding Lecture Material

The following system can help you remember and understand lecture material better and relate information to other things you already know. It consists of three major parts:

▶ Preparing to listen before class

▶ Listening and taking notes during class

▶ Reviewing and recalling information after class

Before Class: Prepare to Remember

Even if lectures don't allow for active participation, you can take a number of active learning steps to make your listening and note-taking more efficient.

Remember that your goals are:

▶ Improved learning in the classroom

▶ A better understanding of what the instructor considers important

▶ A longer attention span

▶ Enhanced retention of information

▶ Clear, well-organized notes for when it's time to study for exams

▶ Better grades

Lectures can be hard to understand if you don't prepare beforehand. You would not want to walk in unprepared to give a speech, interview for a job, plead a case in court, or compete in sports. For each of these situations, you would want to prepare in some way. For the same reason, you should prepare for the lecture by active listening, learning, and remembering.

1. **Do the assigned reading.** Unless you do, you will find the lecturer's comments disjointed, and you may not understand some terms used. Some instructors refer to assigned readings for each class session; others hand out a syllabus and assume you are keeping up with the assigned readings.

   Completing the assigned readings on time will help you listen better and pick out which information is most important when taking notes. Read carefully and take good notes. In books that you own, annotate (add critical or explanatory margin notes), highlight, or underline the text. In books you do not own, such as library books, make a photocopy of the pages and then annotate or highlight.

2. **Pay careful attention to your course syllabus.** Syllabi are formal statements about course expectations, requirements, and procedures. Instructors assume that once students have received their syllabi, they will understand and follow course requirements with few or even no reminders.

3. **Make use of supplementary materials provided by the instructor.** Many professors post lecture outlines or notes to a website prior to class. Download and print these materials for easy reference during class. These materials often provide hints about what the instructor considers most important, and they also can create an organizational structure for note-taking.

4. **Warm up for class.** Before class begins, warm up or preview by reviewing chapter introductions and summaries, referring to related sections in your text and to your notes from the previous class period. This prepares you to pay attention, understand, and remember.

5. **Get organized.** Develop an organizational system. Decide which type of notebook will work best for you. Many study skills' experts suggest using three-ring binders because you can punch holes in syllabi and other course handouts and keep these with class notes. If you prefer using spiral notebooks, consider buying multi-subject notebooks that have pocket dividers for handouts, or be sure to maintain a folder

Confessions of a College Student

Ivan D. Buenrostro

Age: 23

University: Arizona State University

Hometown: Phoenix, Arizona

Major: Aeronautical Management Technology

Favorite book(s): *The Da Vinci Code, The House on Mango Street, Nickel and Dimed, Esperanza's Box of Saints*

Favorite college course: U.S. History, Ethnic Relations

The person who inspires me the most: That would have to be my mom, for her determination and motivation.

Favorite way to relax: Going to the beach, playing the guitar/piano, listening to music, swimming, and hiking

Are you the first to go to college in your family? If so, what impact has that had on your experience? Because I am the first in my family to go to college, I hold myself to high standards because I am setting an example for my two younger siblings. Although I have accomplished many things, I also have enjoyed my college experience. Being the first in my family to attend college has had a positive effect on me. In a way, being the first to go to college has served as additional motivation to achieve what I once viewed as unattainable.

Your proudest moment or biggest accomplishment: My first solo flight

Note-taking confession: To be honest, I used to hate taking notes or going over them to retain more of the material. I figured I could organize thoughts in my head faster than I could by writing them down on paper. You could say I wrote "in between the lines." Rewriting my notes? Why do more work? Although I took plenty of notes in class, they turned out to be virtually useless.

Reading my notes became tedious, so I hardly ever bothered with it, reviewing only a day or two before the exam. Wow, did my grades suffer! What I finally realized was that the material covered in class was only a portion of what I needed to review.

To improve my note-taking, I attended college-sponsored workshops designed to help students take better notes and improve other study skills. All of a sudden, it was the end of the term, with final exam week on top of me. I hadn't studied for a few of my classes and realized that my old note-taking habits really took more of my time than if I had taken neat, organized, and relevant notes in the first place. The class syllabus became a bible for studying. I constantly reviewed the requirements and asked my professors whether they had further suggestions. Slowly I learned to understand their style of teaching. Most importantly, I learned how to take effective notes. In the end, I was able to reduce my study time, and my grades improved dramatically. The only thing I regret is not having discovered note-taking techniques sooner.

for each course. Consider purchasing notebook paper that has a larger left margin for ease in annotating your lecture notes.

During Class: Listen Critically

Listening in class is not like listening to a TV program, listening to a friend, or even listening to a speaker at a meeting. Knowing how to listen in class can help you get more out of what you hear, understand better what you have heard, and save time. Here are some suggestions:

1. **Be ready for the message.** Prepare yourself to hear, to listen, and to receive the message. If you have done the assigned reading, you will know what details are already in the text so that you can focus your note-taking on key concepts during the lecture. You will also know what information is not covered in the text, so you will be prepared to pay closer attention when the instructor is presenting unfamiliar material.

2. **Listen to the main concepts and central ideas, not just to fragmented facts and figures.** Although facts are important, they will be easier to remember and will make more sense when you can place them in a context of concepts, themes, and ideas. You want to understand the material, and only memorizing it won't help you understand it.

3. **Listen for new ideas.** Even if you are an expert on a topic, you can still learn something new. Do not assume that college instructors will present the same information you learned in a similar course in high school.

4. **Repeat mentally.** Words can go in one ear and out the other unless you make an effort to retain them. Think about what you hear and restate it silently in your own words. If you cannot translate the information into your own words, ask for further clarification.

5. **Decide whether what you have heard is not important, somewhat important, or very important.** If it's really not important, let it go. If it's very important, make it a major point in your notes by highlighting or underscoring it, or use it as a major topic in your outline if that is the method you use for note-taking. If it's somewhat important, try to relate it to a very important topic by writing it down as a subset of that topic.

6. **Keep an open mind.** Every class holds the promise of discovering new ideas and uncovering different perspectives. Some professors intentionally present information that challenges your value system. One of the purposes of college is to teach you to think in new and different ways and to learn to provide support for your own beliefs. Instructors want you to think for yourself and do not necessarily expect you to agree with everything they or your classmates say. However, if you want people to respect *your* values and ideas, you must show respect for *theirs* as well by listening with an open mind to what they have to say.

7. **Ask questions.** Early in the term, determine whether the instructor is open to responding to questions during lecture. Some instructors prefer to save questions for the end or to have students ask questions during separate discussion sections or office hours. To some extent, this may depend on the nature of the class, such as large lecture versus small seminar. If your instructor is open to answering questions as they arise, do not hesitate to ask if you did not hear or understand what was said. It is best to clarify what you don't understand immediately, if possible, and other students are likely to have the same questions. If you can't hear another student's question or response, ask that it be repeated.

8. **Sort, organize, and categorize.** When you listen, try to match what you are hearing with what you already know. Take an active role in deciding how best to recall what you are learning.

WIRED WINDOW

YOU WILL DISCOVER many options for using technology to enhance your note-taking skills and your engagement with learning. Some students prefer to bring their laptops to class and either type their notes or use the tablet feature to handwrite their notes into digital files. We think it's important to strike a balance between taking notes on your computer and paying attention to class discussion. Most students can't type as quickly as they can write and need to be much more selective about the information they choose to enter. You might also face a greater challenge extracting the most important points of the lecture or discussion while it is happening. QipIt, a free service, allows you to take pictures of documents, including PowerPoint presentations, whiteboard notes, and overheads, and have them converted to digital documents. If you choose to use such a service, make sure you have obtained permission from your professors to reproduce their notes. Whether you use QipIt or type your own notes in a word processor, it's helpful to organize them so you can find what you are looking for. Assign file names that reflect the content of the notes and the date you took them.

During Class: Take Effective Notes

You can make class time more productive by using your listening skills to take effective notes, but first you have to decide on a system.

Cornell Format One method of organizing notes is called the Cornell format, in which you create a "recall" column on each page of your notebook by drawing a vertical line about two to three inches from the left border. (See Figure 7.1.) You can use the Cornell format in combination with any other format, such as lists, paragraphs, or outlines. As you take notes during lecture—whether just writing down ideas, making lists, or using an outline or paragraph format or some other type of system—write only in the wider column on the right and leave the recall column on the left blank. In the recall column, write down the main ideas and important details as soon after class as possible to aid you when studying for tests.

Outline Format Many students prefer to outline their notes so that key ideas are represented by Roman numerals, while other ideas relating to each key idea are represented in order by uppercase letters, numbers, and lowercase letters. Details, definitions, examples, applications, and explanations can be added to the basic outline. (See Figure 7.2.)

Paragraph Format Writing detailed paragraphs, with each containing a summary of a topic, works well for summarizing what you have read. However, it's hard to summarize a lecture until it is complete, and by that time it may be too late to recall critical information. (See Figure 7.3.)

List Format This format can be effective when taking notes on lists of terms and definitions, facts, or sequences. It is easy to use lists in combination with the Cornell format, with key terms on the left and their definitions and explanations on the right.

	Psychology 101, 1/31/05
	Theories of Personality
Personality trait: define	Personality trait ="durable disposition to behave in a particular way in a variety of situations"
Big 5: Name + describe them	Big 5-McCrae + Costa- (1)extroversion, (or positive emotionality)=outgoing, sociable, friendly, upbeat, assertive,; (2) neuroticism=anxious, hostile, self-conscious, insecure, vulnerable; (3)openness to experience=curiosity, flexibility, imaginative,; (4) agreeableness=sympathetic, trusting, cooperative, modest; (5)conscientiousness=diligent, disciplined, well organized, punctual, dependable
Psychodynamic Theories: Who?	Psychodynamic Theories-focus on unconscious forces Freud-psychoanalysis-3 components of personality-(1)id=primitive, instinctive,
3 components of personality: name and describe	operates according to pleasure principle (immediate gratification); (2)ego=decision-making component, operates according to reality principle (delay gratification until appropriate); (3)superego=moral component, social standards, right + wrong
3 levels of awareness: name and describe	3 levels of awareness-(1) conscious=what one is aware of at a particular moment; (2)preconscious=material just below surface, easily retrieved; (3)unconscious=thoughts, memories, + desires well below surface, but have great influence on behavior

▲ **Figure 7.1** Note-taking in the Cornell Format.

(See Figure 7.4.) Once you have decided on a format for taking notes, you may also want to develop your own system of abbreviations. For example, you might write "inst" instead of *institution* or "eval" instead of *evaluation*.

Write • DISCUSS • Compare • Ask • BLOG • Answer • *Journal*

Describe your current system of note-taking. Does it conform to any of the note-taking methods described above? Is it better, or is it more haphazard?

Psychology 101, 1/31/05: Theories of Personality

I. Personality trait = "durable disposition to behave in a particular way in a variety of situations"

II. Big 5-McCrae + Costa
   A. Extroversion, (or positive emotionality)=outgoing, sociable, friendly, upbeat, assertive
   B. Neuroticism=anxious, hostile, self-conscious, insecure, vulnerable
   C. Openness to experience=curiosity, flexibility, imaginative
   D. Agreeableness=sympathetic, trusting, cooperative, modest
   E. Conscientiousness=diligent, disciplined, well organized, punctual, dependable

III. Psychodynamic Theories-focus on unconscious forces-- Freud—psychoanalysis
   A. 3 components of personality
      1. Id=primitive, instinctive, operates according to pleasure principle (immediate gratification)
      2. Ego=decision-making component, operates according to reality principle (delay gratification until appropriate)
      3. Superego=moral component, social standards, right + wrong
   B. 3 levels of awareness
      1. Conscious=what one is aware of at a particular moment
      2. Preconscious=material just below surface, easily retrieved
      3. Unconscious=thoughts, memories, + desires well below surface, but have great influence on behavior

▲ **Figure 7.2** Note-taking in the Outline Format.

Note-Taking Techniques When taking notes, follow these important steps:

1. **Identify the main ideas.** Well-organized lectures always contain key points. The first principle of effective note-taking is to identify and write down the most important ideas around which the lecture is built. Although supporting details are important as well, focus your note-taking on the main ideas. Such ideas can be buried in details, statistics, anecdotes, or problems, but you will need to identify and record them for further study.

Some instructors announce the purpose of a lecture or offer an outline, thus providing you with the skeleton of main ideas, followed by the details. Others develop

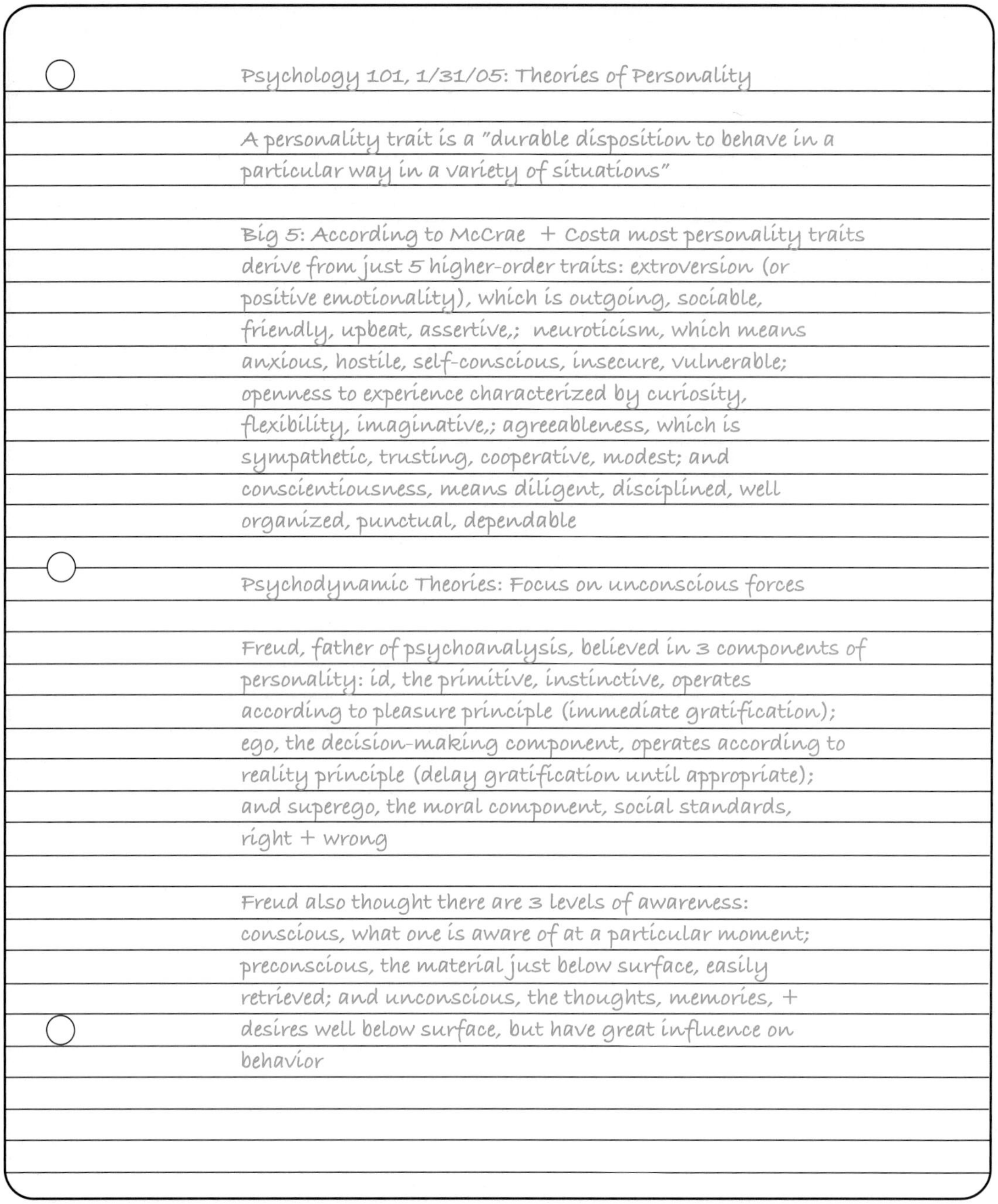

> Psychology 101, 1/31/05: Theories of Personality
>
> A personality trait is a "durable disposition to behave in a particular way in a variety of situations"
>
> Big 5: According to McCrae + Costa most personality traits derive from just 5 higher-order traits: extroversion (or positive emotionality), which is outgoing, sociable, friendly, upbeat, assertive,; neuroticism, which means anxious, hostile, self-conscious, insecure, vulnerable; openness to experience characterized by curiosity, flexibility, imaginative,; agreeableness, which is sympathetic, trusting, cooperative, modest; and conscientiousness, means diligent, disciplined, well organized, punctual, dependable
>
> Psychodynamic Theories: Focus on unconscious forces
>
> Freud, father of psychoanalysis, believed in 3 components of personality: id, the primitive, instinctive, operates according to pleasure principle (immediate gratification); ego, the decision-making component, operates according to reality principle (delay gratification until appropriate); and superego, the moral component, social standards, right + wrong
>
> Freud also thought there are 3 levels of awareness: conscious, what one is aware of at a particular moment; preconscious, the material just below surface, easily retrieved; and unconscious, the thoughts, memories, + desires well below surface, but have great influence on behavior

▲ **Figure 7.3** Note-taking in the Paragraph Format.

overhead transparencies or PowerPoint presentations and perhaps make these materials available on a class website before the lecture. If so, you can enlarge them, print them out, and take notes on the instructor's outline or next to the PowerPoint slides.

Some lecturers change their tone of voice or repeat themselves for each key idea. Some ask questions or promote discussion. If a lecturer says something more than once, chances are it's important. Ask yourself, "What does my instructor want me to know at the end of today's class?"

2. **Don't try to write down everything.** Some first-year students try to do just that. They stop being thinkers and become stenographers. Learn to avoid that trap. If you're an active listener, you will ultimately have shorter but more useful notes. As

Psychology 101, 1/31/05: Theories of Personality

- A personality trait is a "durable disposition to behave in a particular way in a variety of situations"
- Big 5: According to McCrae + Costa most personality traits derive from just 5 higher-order traits
  - extroversion, (or positive emotionality)=outgoing, sociable, friendly, upbeat, assertive
  - neuroticism=anxious, hostile, self-conscious, insecure, vulnerable
  - openness to experience=curiosity, flexibility, imaginative
  - agreeableness=sympathetic, trusting, cooperative, modest
  - conscientiousness=diligent, disciplined, well organized, punctual, dependable
- Psychodynamic Theories: Focus on unconscious forces
- Freud, father of psychoanalysis, believed in 3 components of personality
  - id=primitive, instinctive, operates according to pleasure principle (immediate gratification)
  - ego=decision-making component, operates according to reality principle (delay gratification until appropriate)
  - superego=moral component, social standards, right + wrong
- Freud also thought there are 3 levels of awareness
  - conscious=what one is aware of at a particular moment
  - preconscious=material just below surface, easily retrieved
  - unconscious=thoughts, memories, + desires well below surface, but have great influence on behavior

▲ **Figure 7.4** Note-taking in the List Format.

you take notes, leave spaces so that later you can fill in additional details you might have missed during class. But remember to do so as soon after class as possible. Remember the "forgetting curve": How quickly you forget what you don't write down.

3. **Don't be thrown by a disorganized lecturer.** When a lecture is disorganized, it's your job to try to organize what is said into general and specific frameworks. When the order is not apparent, you'll need to indicate in your notes where the gaps lie. After the lecture, consult your reading material or classmates to fill in these gaps. You might also consult your instructor. Most instructors have regular office hours for student appointments, yet it is amazing how few students use these opportunities for one-on-one interaction. You can also raise questions in class. Asking questions can help your instructor discover which parts of the lecture need more attention and clarification.

Taking Notes in Nonlecture Courses Always be ready to adapt your note-taking methods to match the situation. Group discussion is becoming a popular way to teach in college because it involves active learning. On your campus you may also have Supplemental Instruction (SI) classes that provide further opportunity to discuss the information presented in lectures.

How do you keep a record of what's happening in such classes? Assume you are taking notes in a problem-solving group assignment. You would begin your notes by asking yourself "What is the problem?" and writing down the answer.

As the discussion progresses, you would list the solutions offered. These would be your main ideas. The important details might include the positive and negative aspects of each view or solution. The important thing to remember when taking notes in nonlecture courses is that you need to record the information presented by your classmates as well as by the instructor and to consider all reasonable ideas, even though these might differ from your own.

When a course has separate lecture and discussion sessions, you will need to understand how the discussion sessions relate to and augment the lectures. If different material is covered in lecture or discussion, you may need to ask for guidance in organizing your notes. When similar topics are covered, you can combine your notes so that you have comprehensive, unified coverage of each topic.

How to organize the notes you take in a class discussion depends on the purpose or form of the discussion. But it usually makes good sense to begin with the list of issues or topics that the discussion leader announces. Another approach is to list the questions that the participants raise for discussion. If the discussion is exploring reasons for and against a particular argument, it makes sense to divide your notes into columns or sections for pros and cons. When conflicting views are presented in discussion, it is important to record different perspectives and the rationales behind them. Your instructor may ask you to defend your opinions in light of others' opinions.

After Class: Respond, Recite, Review

Don't let the forgetting curve take its toll on you. As soon after class as possible, review your notes and fill in the details you still remember but missed writing down.

Relate new information to other things you already know. Organize your information. Make a conscious effort to remember. One way is to recite important data to yourself every few minutes. This helps you discover your own reactions and uncover gaps in your comprehension of the material. (Asking and answering questions in class also provides you with the feedback you need to make certain your understanding is accurate.) Now you're ready to embed the major points from your notes in your memory. Use these three important steps for remembering the key points in the lecture:

1. **Write down the main ideas.** For five or ten minutes, quickly review your notes and select key words or phrases that act as labels or tags for main ideas and key information in the notes.

2. **Recite your ideas out loud.** If you don't have a few minutes after class when you can concentrate on reviewing your notes, find some other time during that

same day to review what you have written. You might also want to ask your instructor to glance at your notes to determine whether you have identified the major ideas.

3. **Review the previous day's notes just before the next class session.** As you sit in class the next day waiting for the lecture to begin, use the time to quickly review the notes from the previous day. This will put you in tune with the lecture that is about to begin and also prompt you to ask questions about material from the previous lecture that wasn't clear to you.

These three ways to engage with the material will pay off later when you begin to study for your exams.

What if you have three classes in a row and no time for recall columns or recitations between them? Recall and recite as soon after class as possible. Review the most recent class first. Never delay recall and recitation longer than one day; if you do, it will take you longer to review, make a recall column, and recite. With practice, you can complete your recall column quickly, perhaps between classes, during lunch, or while riding the bus.

Class Notes and Homework Good class notes can help you complete homework assignments. Follow these steps:

1. **Review the homework assignment so that you know what to look for in your notes.**

2. **Skim the notes and put a question mark next to anything you do not understand at first reading.** Draw stars next to topics that warrant special emphasis. Try to place the material in context: What has been going on in the course for the past few weeks? How does today's class fit in?

3. **Do any assigned problems and answer assigned questions.** When you start doing your homework, read each question or problem and ask: What am I supposed to find or find out? Work the problem without referring to your notes or the text, as though you were taking a test. In this way, you will test your knowledge and know when you are prepared for exams.

4. **Persevere.** Don't give up too soon. When you encounter a problem or question that you cannot readily handle, move on only after a reasonable effort. After you have completed the entire assignment, come back to those items that stumped you. Try once more, then take a break. You may need to mull over a particularly difficult problem for several days. Let your unconscious mind have a chance. Inspiration can come while you are waiting for a stoplight or just before you fall asleep.

You may be thinking, "That all sounds good, but who has the time to do all that extra work?" In reality, this approach does work and can actually save you time. Try it for a few weeks and see whether it works for you.

Participating in Class

Learning is not a spectator sport. To really learn, you must talk about what you are learning, write about it, relate it to past experiences, and make what you learn part of yourself. Participation is the heart of active learning. When students speak in class, they are more likely to remember what they have said than what someone else says. So when a professor tosses a question your way or when you have a question to ask, you're actually making it easier to remember the day's lesson.

Naturally, you will be more likely to participate in a class where the instructor emphasizes discussion, calls on students by name, shows students signs of approval and interest, and avoids criticizing you for an incorrect answer. Often answers you and others offer that are not quite correct can lead to new perspectives on a topic.

Unfortunately, large classes often cause instructors to use the lecture method. And large classes can be intimidating. If you speak up in a class of a hundred and think you've made a fool of yourself, you also think that ninety-nine other people know it. Of course, that's somewhat unrealistic. Since you've probably asked a question they were too timid to ask, they'll silently thank you for doing so. If you're lucky, you might even find that the instructor of such a class takes time to ask or answer questions. To take full advantage of these opportunities in all classes, try using these techniques:

1. **Take a seat as close to the front as possible.** If you're seated by name and your name begins with Z, plead bad eyesight or hearing—anything to get moved up front.

2. **Keep your eyes trained on the instructor.** Sitting up front will make this easier for you to do.

3. **Focus on the lecture.** Do not let yourself be distracted. It is wise not to sit near friends who are distracting without meaning to be.

4. **Raise your hand when you don't understand something.** The instructor may answer you immediately, ask you to wait until later in the class, or throw your question to the rest of the class. In each case, you benefit in several ways. The instructor gets to know you, other students get to know you, and you learn from both the instructor and your classmates. But don't overdo it. Both the instructor and your peers will tire of too many questions that disrupt the flow of the class.

5. **Speak up in class.** Ask a question or volunteer to answer a question or make a comment. It becomes easier every time you do this.

6. **Never feel that you're asking a "stupid" question.** If you don't understand something, you have a right to ask for an explanation.

7. **When the instructor calls on you to answer a question, don't bluff.** If you know the answer, give it. If you're not certain, begin with, "I think . . . , but I'm not sure I have it all correct." If you don't know, just say so.

8. **If you've recently read a book or article that is relevant to the class topic, bring it in.** Use it either to ask questions about the subject matter or to provide information that was not covered in class. Next time you have the opportunity, speak up. Class will go by faster, your fellow students and you will get to know one another, your instructor will get to know you, and he or she will in all likelihood be grateful for your participation.

Write • DISCUSS • Compare • Ask • BLOG • Answer • *Journal*

> Do you volunteer questions or comments in your classes? Why or why not? Have you had an experience you remember–either positive or negative– in asking a question or providing a comment in class?

▶ WHERE TO GO FOR HELP

On Campus

Learning Assistance Center Almost every campus has one of these, and this chapter's topics are their specialty. More and more, the best students as well as good students who want to be the best students use learning centers as often as students who are having academic difficulties. These services are offered by both full-time professionals and highly skilled student tutors, all of whom are available at times convenient for you.

Fellow College Students Often the best help you can get is the closest to you: fellow students. But, of course, not just any student will do. Keep an eye out in your classes, residence hall, cocurricular groups, and other places for the most serious, purposeful, and directed students. Those are the ones to seek out.

Join a Study Group Students who do so are much more likely to stay in college and be successful. It does not diminish you in any way to seek assistance from your peers.

Online

The University of St. Thomas maintains this web page that includes links to a variety of study skills tips: http://www.stthomas.edu/academicsupport/helpful_study_skills_links.htm

See guidelines for speaking in class at: http://www.school-for-champions.com/grades/speaking.htm.

Reading and Remembering

In this chapter YOU WILL LEARN

▶ How to preview reading material

▶ How to mark your textbooks

▶ How to review your reading

▶ How to develop a more extensive vocabulary

▶ How to improve your ability to memorize

▶ How experts describe memory and its functions

▶ Why a good memory can be an asset, but isn't all you need to do well in college

© Rhoda Sidney/PhotoEdit

Jeanne L. Higbee of the University of Minnesota-Twin Cities contributed her valuable and considerable expertise to the writing of this chapter.

What Are Your READING AND MEMORY Strategies?

Choose the response that best applies to you:

1 When you are assigned a reading for class, how do you usually begin your reading?

A I sometimes flip through to see whether there will be any interesting topics or pictures I can look forward to.

B I take a look at all of the headings and skim the chapter for material I'm familiar with.

C When I do the reading, I just read from beginning to end—I like to be surprised when I read for my courses.

2 How do you take notes when you read for your courses?

A I sometimes use a highlighter to mark words I should look up.

B I pencil my notes in the margin to summarize what I read in my own words—that helps me remember it and proves to myself I understand what I've read.

C I only skim the reading a few minutes before class and don't have time to make notes.

3 When do you review your reading from class?

A Right away, if it's something I'm interested in; if I'm not interested, I just force myself to look at it again right before the exam.

B Once a week—I designate a day to go over readings to be sure they are fresh in my head.

C Never—I read it once, so there's nothing else to go over.

4 Why do you think professors assign readings for your courses?

A So we have something to talk about in class, and they can test us on it.

B So that they can refer to readings during class and have students expand their knowledge on the subject.

C So they can keep students busy.

5 Do you use strategies for organizing information that help you remember it better?

A However the instructor presents the material is how it's organized for me—they've already done the work so why should I reorganize it?

B I organize my notes after each class so that I can connect and remember information that is presented.

C Sometimes I'll put all the keywords, phrases, or dates together and review them, but that strategy doesn't work for all my classes.

Review your responses. **A** responses indicate that you have some idea of how to read effectively for class, but in order to do your best, you'll need to improve. **B** responses indicate that you have a good idea of how to read and comprehend course material. **C** responses indicate that you need to develop a better understanding of reading strategies to do well in college classes. Wherever you are in your current understanding, this chapter will help you learn more about why reading is a basic strategy for success in the classroom.

This chapter covers two important aspects of college success: reading and remembering. Your ability to read with understanding and to concentrate while you read will determine whether you succeed in your courses. And, of course, remembering what you read as well as what you hear in lectures and class discussions is the key to learning. In fact, there is no learning without memory. What makes reading and remembering the material in college textbooks especially challenging? College textbooks, unlike most books you read for pleasure, are loaded with concepts, terms, and complex information that you are expected to learn on your own in a short period of time. To do this, you will need to learn and use reading and memory methods such as those in this chapter.

A Simple Plan for Textbook Reading

The following plan for textbook reading can pay off. It is designed to increase your focus and concentration, promote greater understanding of what you read, and prepare you to study for tests and exams. This system is based on four steps: previewing, reading, marking, and reviewing.

Previewing

The purpose of previewing is to get the big picture, to understand how what you are about to read is connected to what you already know and to the material the instructor is covering in class. Begin by reading the title of the chapter. Ask yourself, "What do I already know about this subject?" Next, quickly read through the introductory paragraphs, then read the summary at the beginning or end of the chapter (if one is there). Finally, take a few minutes to skim through the chapter headings and subheadings. Note any study exercises at the end of the chapter.

As part of your preview, note how many pages the chapter contains. It's a good idea to decide in advance how many pages you can reasonably expect to cover in your first fifty-minute study period. This can help build your concentration as you work toward your goal of reading a specific number of pages. Before long, you'll know how many pages are practical for you.

Keep in mind that different types of textbooks require more or less time to read. For example, depending on your interests and previous knowledge, you may be able to read a psychology textbook more quickly than a logic textbook that presents a whole new symbol system.

Mapping

Mapping the chapter as you preview it provides a visual guide to how different chapter ideas fit together. Because about 75 percent of students identify themselves as visual learners, visual mapping is an excellent learning tool for test preparation as well as reading. How do you map a chapter? While you are previewing, use either a wheel or a branching structure. (See Figure 8.1.) In the wheel structure, place

Wheel Map

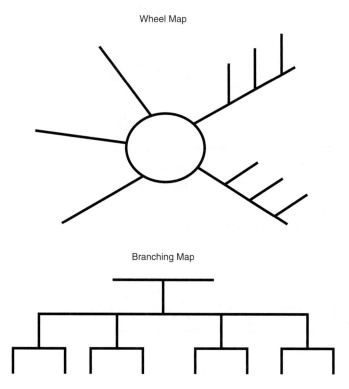

Branching Map

◀ **Figure 8.1** Wheel and Branching Maps

the central idea of the chapter in the circle. The central idea should be found in the introduction to the chapter and can also be apparent in the chapter title. Then place secondary ideas on the spokes emanating from the circle, and place offshoots of those ideas on the lines attached to the spokes. In the branching map, the main idea goes at the top, followed by supporting ideas on the second tier, and so forth. Fill in the title first.

Then, as you skim through the rest of the chapter, use the headings and subheadings to fill in the key ideas.

Reading Your Textbook

Annotate   Try a strategy known as annotating the text. In your own words, write key ideas in the margins of the text.

Learn to Concentrate   Many factors affect your ability to concentrate and understand texts: the time of day, your energy level, your interest in the material, and your study location. Some things to do to help you concentrate include finding a study

▶ **Reading enriches your college experience.**

location that is removed from traffic and distracting noises; jotting study questions in the margin, taking notes, or reciting key ideas; and setting goals for your study period, such as "I will read twenty pages of my psychology textbook in the next fifty minutes." These are just a few things you can do. Can you think of others to help you improve your concentration?

Marking Your Textbook Think a moment about your goals for making marks in your own textbooks. Some students report that *marking* is an active reading strategy that helps them focus and concentrate on the material as they read. In addition, most students expect to use their text notations when studying for tests. To meet these goals, some students like to underline, some prefer to highlight, and others use margin notes or annotations. Figure 8.2 provides an example of each method. No matter which method you prefer, remember these two important guidelines:

1. **Read before you mark.** Finish reading a section before you decide which are the most important ideas and concepts. Mark only those ideas, using your preferred methods (highlighting, underlining, circling key terms, or annotating).

2. **Think before you mark.** When you read a text for the first time, everything can seem important. Only after you have completed a section and reflected on it will you be ready to identify the key ideas. Ask yourself, "What are the most important ideas? What will I see on the test?" This can help you avoid marking too much material.

Two other considerations can affect your decisions regarding textbook marking. First, if you just make notes or underline directly on the pages of your textbook, you are committing yourself to at least one more viewing of all the pages you have already read—all 400 pages of your anatomy or art history textbook. A more productive use of your time would be taking notes, creating flash cards, making lists, or outlining textbook chapters. These methods are also more practical if you intend to review with a friend or study group.

Second, sometimes highlighting or underlining can provide you with a false sense of security. You may have determined what is most important, but you have not necessarily tested yourself on your understanding of the material.

When you force yourself to put something in your own words while taking notes, you are not only predicting exam questions but also assessing whether you can answer them. Although these active reading strategies take more time initially, they can save you time in the long run because they not only promote concentration as you read but also make it easy to review. So you probably won't have to pull an all-nighter before an exam.

Reading to Question, to Interpret, and to Understand An important step in textbook reading is to monitor your comprehension. As you read, ask yourself, "Do I understand this?" If not, stop and reread the material. Look up words that are not clear. Try to clarify the main points and how they relate to one another.

Another way to check comprehension is to try to recite the material aloud to yourself or your study partner. Using a study group to monitor your comprehension gives you immediate feedback and is highly motivating. One way that group members can

CONCEPT CHECKS

7. *Some students who read a chapter slowly get very good grades; others get poor grades. Why?*

8. *Most actors and public speakers who have to memorize lengthy passages spend little time simply repeating the words and more time thinking about them. Why? (Check your answers on page 288.)*

People need to monitor their understanding of a text to decide whether to keep studying or whether they already understand it well enough. Most readers have trouble making that judgment correctly.

SELF-MONITORING OF UNDERSTANDING

Whenever you are studying a text, you periodically have to decide, "Should I keep on studying this section, or do I already understand it well enough?" Most students have trouble monitoring their own understanding. In one study, psychology instructors asked their students before each test to guess whether they would do better or worse on that test than they usually do. Students also guessed after each test whether they had done better or worse than usual. Most students' guesses were no more accurate than chance (Sjostrom & Marks, 1994). Such inaccuracy represents a problem: Students who do not know how well they understand the material will make bad judgments about when to keep on studying and when to quit.

Even when you are reading a single sentence, you have to decide whether you understand the sentence or whether you should stop and reread it. Here is a sentence once published in the student newspaper at North Carolina State University:

He said Harris told him she and Brothers told French that grades had been changed.

Ordinarily, when good readers come to such a confusing sentence, they notice their own confusion and reread the sentence or, if necessary, the whole paragraph. Poor readers tend to read at their same speed for both easy and difficult materials; they are less likely than good readers to slow down when they come to difficult sentences.

Although monitoring one's own understanding is difficult and often inaccurate, it is not impossible. For example, suppose I tell you that you are to read three chapters dealing with, say, thermodynamics, the history of volleyball, and the Japanese stock market.

(why)

(How)

Later you will take tests on each chapter. Before you start reading, predict your approximate scores on the three tests. Most people make a guess based on how much they already know about the three topics. If we let them read the three chapters and again make a guess about their test performances, they do in fact make more accurate predictions than they did before reading (Maki & Serra, 1992). That improvement indicates some ability to monitor one's own understanding of a text.

A systematic way to monitor your own understanding of a text is the (SPAR) method: *Survey, Process* meaningfully, *Ask* questions, and *Review* and test yourself. Start with an overview of what a passage is about, read it carefully, and then see whether you can answer questions about the passage or explain it to others. If not, go back and reread.

SPAR
Survey
Process
Ask
Review

Also decide about larger units?

THE TIMING OF STUDY

Other things being equal, people tend to remember recent experiences better than earlier experiences. For example, suppose someone reads you a list of 20 words and asks you to recall as many of them as possible. The list is far too long for you to recite from your phonological loop; however, you should be able to remember at least a few. Typically, people remember items at the beginning and end of the list better than they remember those in the middle.

That tendency, known as the **serial-order effect**, includes two aspects: The *primacy effect* is the tendency to remember the first items; the *recency effect* refers to the tendency to remember the last items. One explanation for the primacy effect is that the listener gets to rehearse the first few items for a few moments alone with no interference from the others. One explanation for the recency effect is that the last items are still in

Cause of primacy effect

▲ **Figure 8.2** Sample Marked Pages

the listener's phonological loop at the time of the test.

Cause of recency effect

The phonological loop cannot be the whole explanation for the recency effect, however. In one study, British rugby players were asked to name the teams they had played against in the current season. Players were most likely to remember the last couple of teams they had played against, thus showing a clear recency effect even though they were recalling events that occurred weeks apart (Baddeley & Hitch, 1977). (The phonological loop holds information only for a matter of seconds.)

So, studying material—or, rather, *reviewing* material—shortly before a test is likely to improve recall. Now let's consider the opposite: Suppose you studied something years ago and have not reviewed it since then. For example, suppose you studied a foreign language in high school several years ago. Now you are considering taking a college course in the language, but you are hesitant because you are sure you have forgotten it all. Have you?

Harry Bahrick (1984) tested people who had studied Spanish in school 1 to 50 years previously. Nearly all agreed that they had rarely used Spanish and had not refreshed their memories at all since their school days. (That is a disturbing comment, but beside the point.) Their retention of Spanish dropped noticeably in the first 3 to 6 years, but remained fairly stable from then on (Fig-

ure 7.18). In other words, we do not completely forget even very old memories that we seldom use.

In a later study, Bahrick and members of his family studied foreign-language vocabulary either on a moderately frequent basis (practicing once every 2 weeks) or on a less frequent basis (as seldom as once every 8 weeks), and tested their knowledge years later. The result: More frequent study led to faster learning; however, less frequent study led to better long-term retention, measured years later (Bahrick, Bahrick, Bahrick, & Bahrick, 1993).

The principle here is far more general than just the study of foreign languages. *If you want to remember something well for a test,* your best strategy is to study it as close as possible to the time of the test, in order to take advantage of the recency effect and decrease the effects of retroactive interference. Obviously, I do not mean that you should wait until the night before the test to start studying, but you might rely on an extensive review at that time. You should also, ideally, study under conditions similar to the conditions of the test. For example, you might study in the same room where the test will be given, or at the same time of day.

However, *if you want to remember something long after the test is over,* then the advice I have just given you is all wrong. To be able to remember something whenever you want, wherever you are, and whatever you are doing, you should study it under as varied circumstances as possible. Study and review at various times and places with long, irregular intervals between study sessions. Studying under such inconsistent conditions will slow down your original learning, but it will improve your ability to recall it long afterwards (Schmidt & Bjork, 1992).

Studying for test vs. studying for long term

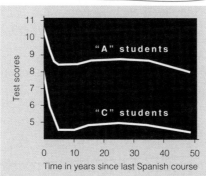

FIGURE 7.18
(Left) Spanish vocabulary as measured by a recognition test shows a rapid decline in the first few years but then long-term stability. (From Bahrick, 1984.) (Right) Within a few years after taking your last foreign-language course, you may think you have forgotten it all. You have not, and even the part you have forgotten will come back (through relearning) if you visit a country where you can practice the language.

CHAPTER 7
MEMORY

284

▲ **Figure 8.2** Continued

© Don Smetzer/PhotoEdit

work together is to divide up a chapter for previewing and studying and get together later to teach the material to one another.

Recycle Your Reading After you have read and marked or taken notes on key ideas from the first section of the chapter, proceed to each subsequent section until you have finished the chapter.

After you have completed each section—and *before* you move on to the next section—ask again, "What are the key ideas? What will I see on the test?" At the end of each section, try to guess what information the author will present in the next section. Good reading should lead you from one section to the next, with each new section adding to your understanding.

Reviewing

The final step in effective textbook reading is reviewing. Many students expect the improbable—that they will read through their text material one time and be able to remember the ideas four, six, or even twelve weeks later at test time. More realistically, you will need to include regular reviews in your study process. Here is where your notes, study questions, annotations, flash cards, visual maps, and outlines are most useful. Your study goal should be to review the material from each chapter every week.

Consider ways to use your many senses to review. Recite aloud. Tick off each item in a list on each of your fingertips. Post diagrams, maps, or outlines around your living space so that you will see them often and will be likely to visualize them while taking the test.

Confessions of a College Student

Marisa F. Rodriguez

Age: 30

College: Pima Community College

Hometown: Tucson, Arizona

Major: Business, Finance

Favorite book(s): *My Sister's Keeper, The House of the Spirits*

Favorite college course: Writing

The person who inspires me the most or whom I would most like to meet: My kids inspire me the most.

Heroes: My mom and my grandma

Favorite way to relax: Reading a good book

Your proudest moment or biggest accomplishment: I would have to say that having my children were my proudest moments as well as my biggest accomplishments to date. I plan to add graduating from college to this list.

Favorite food: Lasagna

Reading strategies confession: I find college texts difficult to read because the information they contain isn't always something that is particularly interesting to me. As a result, I find myself procrastinating. Yet I know the reading is important to my studies, so I have to get through it. To help myself through this difficulty, I first skim the material and only read the portions that interest me. Then I go through the material again later in more detail, this time taking notes. Writing down important details helps me remember things more solidly than if I just read the material and try to memorize it. I find that talking to myself out loud helps me work through particularly difficult areas of the reading. I put the text in my own words so I can relate to the reading and therefore make it easier to remember.

Reading the text for each course is crucial to your college education. Each chapter of your text contains information your instructors might use in their lectures. By reading the text before the lectures, you will better understand what they say. You will also be able to ask informed questions.

Write • DISCUSS • Compare • Ask • BLOG • Answer • Journal

> Think about your college textbooks for a moment. Which of them is the hardest for you to read and comprehend? Which is the easiest? How are these books different in content, appearance, and interest to you? Are they different from your high school texts? If so, how?

Adjusting Your Reading Style

With effort you can improve your reading dramatically, but remember to be flexible. How you read depends on the material. Assess the relative importance and difficulty of the assigned readings, and adjust your reading style and the time you allot accordingly. Connect one important idea to another by asking yourself, "Why am I reading this? Where does this fit in?" When the textbook material is virtually identical to the lecture material, you can save time by concentrating mainly on one or the other. It takes a planned approach to read textbook materials and other assigned readings with good understanding and recall.

Developing Your Vocabulary

Textbooks are full of new terminology. In fact, one could argue that learning chemistry is largely a matter of learning the language of chemists and that mastering philosophy or history or sociology requires a mastery of the terminology of each particular *discipline*.

If words are such a basic and essential component of knowledge, what is the best way to learn them? Follow these basic vocabulary-building strategies:

▶ During your overview of the chapter, notice and jot down unfamiliar terms. Consider making a flash card for each term or making a list.

▶ When you encounter challenging words, consider the context. See whether you can predict the meaning of an unfamiliar term using the surrounding words.

▶ If context by itself is not enough, try analyzing the term to discover the root, or base part, or other meaningful parts of the word. For example, *emissary* has the root "to emit" or "to send forth," so you can guess that an emissary is someone sent forth with a message. Similarly, note prefixes and suffixes. For example, *anti-* means "against" and *pro-* means "for."

▶ Use the glossary of this textbook, a dictionary, or http://www.m-w.com/netdict.htm (*The Merriam-Webster Dictionary Online*) to locate the definition.

▶ Note any multiple definitions and search for the meaning that fits this usage.

▶ Take every opportunity to use these new terms in your writing and speaking. If you use a new term, then you'll know it! In addition, studying new terms on flash cards or study sheets can be handy at exam time.

If English Is Not Your First Language

The English language is one of the most difficult languages to learn. Words are often spelled differently than the way they sound, and the language is full of *idioms*— phrases that are peculiar and cannot be understood from the individual meanings of the words. For example, if you are "under the gun," that means you are under intense pressure to do something. If you are a non-native English speaker and are having trouble reading your textbooks, reading slowly and reading more than once can help you improve your comprehension. Make sure that you have two good dictionaries— one in English and one that links English with your primary language—and look up the words that you don't know. Be sure to practice thinking, writing, and speaking in English, and take advantage of your college's helping services. Your campus may have ESL (English as a Second Language) tutoring and workshops. Ask your advisor or your first-year seminar instructor to help you locate those services.

Memory and Learning

It's easy for people to blame their difficulty in remembering what they read or hear on the way they live—multitasking has become the norm for college students and instructors. Admittedly, it's hard to focus on anything for very long if your life is full of daily distractions and competing responsibilities, or if you're not getting the sleep you need. Have you ever read a page or two of your text and then realized that you couldn't remember a word of what you had read? Or have you ever had the experience of walking into a room with a particular task in mind and immediately forgetting what that task was? In either case, you were probably interrupted either by your own thoughts or by someone or something else. Have you ever felt the panic that comes from blanking on a test, even though you studied hard and thought you knew the material? It could have been that because you pulled an all-nighter studying, exhaustion raised your stress level and caused your mind to go blank. Such experiences happen to everyone at one time or another. But obviously to do well in college—and in life—it's important that you improve your ability to remember what you're reading, hearing, and experiencing. Although there is no learning without memory, not all memory involves real learning.

Is a good memory all you need to do well in college? Most memory strategies tend to focus on helping you remember names, dates, numbers, vocabulary, graphic materials, formulas—the bits and pieces of knowledge. Although it's important to be able to remember specific bits of information, it is even more important to develop a deep understanding of course material. If you know the date the Civil War began and the fort where the first shots were fired, but you don't really know *why* the Civil War was fought, you're missing the point of a college education. College is about *deep learning*, understanding the why and how behind the details. So don't forget that even though recall of specific facts is certainly *necessary*, it isn't *sufficient*. In order to do well in college courses, you need to understand major themes and ideas. And you also need to hone your ability to think critically about what you're learning.

How Memory Works

Kenneth Higbee describes two different processes involved in memory. The first is *short-term memory*, defined as how many items you are able to perceive at one time. Higbee writes that information stored in short-term memory is forgotten in less than thirty seconds (and sometimes much faster) unless you take action to either keep that information in short-term memory—for example, writing the information down or moving it to *long-term memory*.[1]

---

[1] Kenneth L. Higbee, *Your Memory: How It Works and How to Improve It*, 2nd rev. ed. (New York: Marlowe & Co., 2001).

Although short-term memory is significantly limited, it has a number of uses. It serves as an immediate but temporary holding tank for information. It helps you maintain a reasonable attention span so you can keep track of topics mentioned in conversation, and it enables you to stay on task with the goals you are pursuing at any moment. But even these simple functions of short-term memory fail on occasion. If the telephone rings, if someone asks you a question, if you're interrupted in any way, you will find that your attention suffers and that you essentially have to start over in reconstructing short-term memory.

The second memory process is *long-term memory*, which is the type of memory you need to improve in order to remember what you're learning in college. Long-term memory can be described in three ways: *procedural*, remembering how to do something, such as solving a mathematical problem or playing a musical instrument; *semantic*, remembering facts and meanings without remembering where and when you learned those things; and *episodic*, remembering particular events, their time and place.[2]

You are using your procedural memory when you get on a bicycle you haven't ridden in years, when you can recall the first piece you learned to play on the piano, or when you effortlessly type a letter or class report. Your semantic memory is used continuously to recall word meanings or important dates, such as your mother's or father's birthday. Episodic memory allows you to remember events in which you were involved: a vacation, your first day in school, the moment you opened your acceptance letter from your college or university. Some people can recall not only the event but also the very date and time the event happened. For others, although the event stands out, the dates and times are harder to remember immediately.

Strategies for Improving Your Memory

The benefits of having a good memory are obvious. In college, your memory will help you retain information and ace tests. After college, the ability to recall names, procedures, presentations, and appointments will save you energy, time, and a lot of embarrassment.

There are many ways to go about remembering. Have you ever had to memorize a speech or lines from a play? How you approach committing the lines to memory depends on your learning style. If you're an aural learner, you might choose to record your lines as well as the lines of other characters and listen to them on tape. If you're a visual learner, you can best remember by visualizing where your lines appear on the page in the script. If you learn best by reading, you will simply read and reread the script over and over, and if you're a kinesthetic learner, you perhaps need to walk or move across an imaginary stage while you're reading the script.

Can you apply similar approaches to remembering material for an exam? Perhaps you can. But although knowing specific words will help, remembering concepts

[2] W. F. Brewer and J. R. Pani, "The Structure of Human Memory," in *The Psychology of Learning and Motivation: Advances in Research and Theory*, ed. G. H. Bower, 17 (New York: Academic Press, 1983), 1–38.

and ideas is much more important. To embed such ideas in your mind, ask yourself these questions as you review your notes and books:

1. What is the essence of the idea?

2. Why does the idea make sense—what is the logic behind it?

3. How does this idea connect with other ideas in the material?

4. What might be arguments against the idea?

Specific Aids to Memory

The human mind has discovered ingenious ways to remember information. Here are some specific methods that can be useful to you as you're trying to nail down the causes of World War I, trying to remember the steps in a chemistry problem, or absorbing a mathematical formula.

1. **Pay attention to what you're hearing or reading.** This suggestion is perhaps the most basic and the most important. If you're sitting in class thinking about everything except what the professor is saying, your memory doesn't have a chance. If you're reading and you find your mind wandering, you're wasting your study time. So force yourself to focus.

2. **Don't rely on studying just once before an exam.** Read and review class material many times starting just after each class. The more often you review, the more likely the material will be imprinted on your brain.

3. **Overlearn the material.** After you know and think you understand the material you're studying, go over it again to make sure that you'll retain it for a long time. Test yourself or ask someone else to test you. Recite aloud what you're trying to remember in your own words.

4. **Check out the Internet.** If you're having trouble remembering what you have learned, Google a keyword and try to find interesting details that engage you in learning more, not less, about the subject. Many first-year courses cover such a large amount of material that you'll miss the more interesting details—unless you seek them out for yourself. And as your interest increases, so will your memory.

5. **Study in groups.** Although group study has far broader benefits than improving your memory, working with others on difficult material is a great way to remember more of the content. Group members can test each other and challenge each other's interpretation of the material. Group members can think together about creative or even silly ways to remember.

6. **Be sure you have the big picture.** Whenever you begin a course, make sure that you're clear on what the course will cover. You can talk with someone who has already taken the course or you can take a brief look at all the reading assignments. Having the big picture helps you remember the details of what you're learning.

7. **Look for connections between your life and what's going on in your courses.** College courses may seem irrelevant to you, but actually, if you look, you'll find many connections between course material and your daily life. Seeing those connections will make your course work more interesting and help you remember what you're learning. For example, if you're taking a music theory course and studying chord patterns, listen for those patterns in contemporary music. Many pop songs are built around a 1-4-5-1 chord sequence. Can you recognize them?

8. Analyze how you study and remember best. How are you more likely to remember what you hear, what you read, what you sing, or what you do? If you learn best by listening, record class lectures and replay them. If it's easy for you to remember songs, put your class notes to music. If you need to be *doing* something in order to remember, stand up or sit on the edge of your chair, walk around, or gesture with your arms while you read and recite. Exerting energy while you study will keep you alert.

9. Work around what you are trying to remember. If your memory is stuck, try to remember words or concepts that are related. Brainstorm with yourself everything you know about that concept or person, and it is likely you'll be able to remember the specific information you've temporarily forgotten.

Write • DISCUSS • Compare • Ask • BLOG • Answer • *Journal*

Do you have a particular technique or strategy for remembering bits and pieces of information, such as reciting them over and over or making up silly songs or rhymes? What technique works for you?

10. Take notes on your notes. Some people find they study best by writing and rewriting. Rewriting the most important themes in your notes and taking additional notes on your reading material will help you remember what's most important.

11. Get organized. If your desk or your computer is organized, you'll spend less time trying to remember a file name or where you put a particular document. And as you rewrite your notes, putting them in a logical order that makes sense to you will help you remember them.

12. Find the right atmosphere for studying and remembering. Where do you concentrate most effectively—at your home, in your residence hall, in the library? Whatever the space, you need a quiet location where you will not be distracted. Some people concentrate best in absolute quiet; others seem to benefit from some soft background music (instrumental). But don't fool yourself. Studying in bed, in front of the TV, or while listening to loud music (or loud friends) can be a waste of your study time.

13. Avoid pre-exam all-nighters. You may hear your friends bragging about pulling an all-nighter before an exam. But last-minute cramming, especially when it deprives you of sleep, is probably the worst thing you can do if you want to remember what you've read.

14. Say it over and over. Probably the most time-tested memory technique is reciting whatever you're trying to remember over and over out loud. Talking out loud is particularly important and is more effective than reciting in your head. This means that occasionally you'll need to find a study location where you're alone and won't bother others when you're talking to yourself.

15. Reduce stressors in your life. Although there's no way to determine how much worry or stress causes you to forget, most people agree that stress can be a distraction. Healthy, stress-reducing behaviors, such as meditation, exercise, and sleep, are especially important for college students. Many campuses have counseling or health centers that can provide resources to help you deal with whatever might be causing stress in your daily life.

▶ WHERE TO GO FOR HELP

On Campus

Learning Assistance Center Most campuses have one of these, and reading assistance is one of their specialties. The best students, good students who want to be the best students, and students with academic difficulties all use learning centers. These services are offered by both full-time professionals and highly skilled student tutors.

Fellow College Students Often the best help you can get is the closest to you. Keep an eye out in your classes, residence hall, out-of-class clubs and activities, and so forth for the best students—those who appear the most serious, purposeful, and directed. Hire a tutor. Join a study group. Students who do these things are much more likely to be successful.

Online

Middle Tennessee State University: http://www.mtsu.edu/~studskl/Txtbook.html. This page offers advice for better textbook reading.

This web page from Niagara University includes many links to other websites with a variety of study strategies: http://www.niagara.edu/oas/learning_center/study_reading_strategies/reading.htm

Review of the Research on Memory and College Student Learning: http://www.ferris.edu/HTMLS/academics/center/Teaching_and_Learning_Tips/Memory/indexMemory.htm. This website is designed for instructors; however, it includes lots of interesting information for students as well.

Memorization techniques: http://www.accd.edu/sac/history/keller/ACCDitg/SSMT.htm. The Alamo Community College District maintains this excellent website.

Doing Your Best on Exams and Tests

In this chapter YOU WILL LEARN

▶ Ways to prepare yourself physically, emotionally, and academically for exams

▶ How to devise a study plan for an exam

▶ How to reduce test anxiety

▶ What to do during the exam

▶ How to take different types of tests

▶ How cheating hurts you, your friends, and your college or university

Jeanne L. Higbee of the University of Minnesota-Twin Cities contributed her valuable and considerable expertise to the writing of this chapter.

How Well Do YOU TAKE EXAMS and TESTS?

Read the following questions and choose the answer that fits you best.

1 *When do you begin studying for a test or examination?*

Ⓐ I try to study as I go along so I don't have to cram before an exam. A few days before the exam, I review all my notes and reading.

Ⓑ I think I learn best under pressure, so I wait until the night before the exam.

Ⓒ I try to keep up with my reading and reviews, but I still do last-minute cram sessions.

2 *Do you usually know what to expect on a test before you take it?*

Ⓐ I make sure I know the test format and what exactly we'll be tested on so that I'm not surprised the day of the exam.

Ⓑ No, I like to be surprised—I work well under pressure.

Ⓒ Sometimes—I assume math and science exams will be multiple choice and that English and history exams will be essay format, although I'm not always right.

3 *When presented with an essay question on an exam, what do you do?*

Ⓐ I pinpoint keywords so I'm sure I know what the question is asking me and then formulate an outline of my answer to help organize my thoughts.

Ⓑ I begin writing my answer immediately and ramble on until I've gotten everything down I know about the topic.

Ⓒ If I don't know the answer, I might panic; but if I do, I can usually get through the question somewhat coherently.

4 *What do you do when you finish an exam early?*

Ⓐ I like to look over my answers to be sure I didn't make any silly mistakes on multiple choice exams and to clean up any writing errors on essay exams.

Ⓑ Hand it in and get out of there—I'm just glad it's over!

Ⓒ I get a little nervous when I'm the first person in the class to finish, and I will look over my exam until someone else turns in theirs. Then I'll turn mine in.

5 *How would you react if a classmate asked you about purchasing a paper over the Internet?*

Ⓐ I would advise my classmate not to do this. The risks are too great, and if you use someone else's work, you don't learn anything yourself.

Ⓑ I'd share a couple of sites I've found. I think you have to help your friends.

Ⓒ I really don't know what I'd do. I don't think it's a good idea because you might get caught.

Review your responses. Ⓐ responses indicate that you are prepared to do well on exams and tests in college and that you understand some basic guidelines to avoid plagiarism. Ⓑ responses indicate that you haven't really thought much about how to prepare effectively. Ⓒ responses indicate that you have some understanding of what you need to do to prepare, but you need to improve your skills in order to do your best on exams. Whatever your responses, this chapter will help you learn more about this important preparation skill that you will use while you're in college and in life beyond.

Throughout your college career and your life after college, instructors and employers will periodically evaluate your knowledge and skills. Although employers use your actual job performance as their primary means of evaluation, college instructors most often use written or oral tests and examinations. In some of your courses, evaluation will be done frequently in the form of homework, weekly or biweekly tests, and cumulative examinations. In others, you will find that your final grade will depend only on a midterm and final examination. Although test taking isn't most students' favorite activity, doing your best is critically important to your success in college.

Although you can prepare for exams in many ways, we have found that certain methods are more effective than others. The methods we suggest will help you understand the big picture—the reasons, arguments, and assumptions on which your answers are based. In addition, these methods will also help you remember the essential details so you can perform well on both essay exams and multiple-choice tests. As you become a better test taker, you will find that you actually learn more and, as an added benefit, you experience less test anxiety.

Studying for Tests

If you consistently use good study techniques, you will process and learn most of what you need to know for a test long before the actual test date. But just before a scheduled test or examination, you'll need to focus your study efforts on the most challenging concepts, practice recalling information, and familiarize yourself with details. One of the best ways to prepare for an exam is to join a study group. Group members will have different views of the instructor's goals and objectives and can quiz each other on important facts and concepts.

Review Sheets, Mind Maps, and Other Tools

To prepare for an exam covering large amounts of material, you need to condense the volume of notes and text pages into manageable study units. Review your materials with these questions in mind: Is this one of the key ideas in the chapter or unit? Will you see this on the test? You may prefer to highlight, underline, or annotate the most important ideas or to create outlines, lists, or visual maps containing key ideas.

Use your notes to develop *review sheets*. Make lists of key terms and ideas (from the recall column, if you've used the Cornell method) that you need to remember. Also, do not underestimate the value of using the recall column from your lecture notes to test yourself or others on information presented in class.

A *mind map* is essentially a review sheet with a visual element. Its word and visual patterns provide you with highly charged clues to jog your memory. Because they are visual, mind maps help many students recall information more easily.

Figure 9.1 shows what a mind map might look like for a chapter on listening and learning in the classroom. See whether you can reconstruct the ideas in the chapter by following the connections in the map. Then make a visual mind map for this chapter, and see how much more you can remember after studying it a number of times.

In addition to review sheets and mind maps, you may want to create *flash cards*. One of the advantages of flash cards is that you can keep them in an outside pocket of your backpack and pull them out to study anywhere, even when you don't have enough time to pull out your notebook to study. Also, you always know where you left off. Flash cards can assist you in making good use of time that otherwise would be wasted, like time spent on the bus or waiting for a friend.

Summaries

Writing summaries of class topics can be helpful in preparing for essay and short-answer exams. By condensing the main ideas into a concise written summary, you

▲ **Figure 9.1** Sample Mind Map on Listening and Learning in the Classroom

store information in your long-term memory so you can retrieve it to answer an essay question. Here's how:

1. Predict a test question from your lecture notes or other materials.

2. Read the chapter, supplemental articles, notes, or other resources. Underline or mark main ideas as you go, make notations, or outline on a separate sheet of paper.

3. Analyze and abstract. What is the purpose of the material? Does it compare, define a concept, or prove an idea? What are the main ideas? How would you explain the material to someone else?

4. Make connections between main points and key supporting details. Reread to identify each main point and supporting evidence. Create an outline to assist you in this process.

5. Select, condense, order. Review underlined material and begin putting the ideas in your own words. Number in a logical order what you underlined or highlighted.

6. Write your ideas precisely in a draft. In the first sentence, state the purpose of your summary. Follow with each main point and its supporting ideas. See how much of the draft you can develop from memory without relying on your notes.

7. Review your draft. Read it over, adding missing transitions or insufficient information. Check the logic of your summary. Annotate with the material you used for later reference.

8. Test your memory. Put your draft away and try to recite the contents of the summary to yourself out loud, or explain it to a study partner who can provide feedback on the information you have omitted.

9. Schedule time to review summaries, and double-check your memory shortly before the test. You may want to do this with a partner, although some students prefer to review alone. Some faculty members will also be open to assisting you in this process and providing feedback on your summaries.

Overcoming Test Anxiety

Test anxiety takes many different forms and has many sources. It can be the result of pressure that students put on themselves to succeed. Some stress connected with taking exams is natural and can enhance performance. However, when students put too much pressure on themselves, stress is no longer motivating but debilitating.

The expectations of parents, a spouse, friends, and other people who are close to you can also induce test anxiety. Sometimes, for example, students who are the first in their families to attend college bear on their shoulders the weight of generations before them who have not had this opportunity. The pressure can be overwhelming.

Finally, some test anxiety is caused by lack of preparation, such as by not keeping up with assigned reading, homework, and other academic commitments. Procrastination can begin a downward spiral because after you do poorly on the first test in a course, there is even more pressure to do well on future tests. This situation becomes even more difficult if the units of the course build on one another, as in math and foreign languages. While you are trying to master the new material after the test, you are still trying to catch up on the old material as well.

▲ **Sometimes test anxiety can cause you to forget what you have learned.**

Types of Test Anxiety Students who experience test anxiety under some circumstances do not necessarily feel it in all testing situations. For example, you may do fine on classroom tests but feel anxious during standardized examinations like the SAT and ACT. Attending preparation workshops and taking practice exams not only can better prepare you for standardized tests but can also help you overcome your anxiety.

Some students are only anxious about certain types of classroom tests such as essay exams. If you fear essay exams, try predicting the questions and writing sample essays by yourself or with others in a study group.

Some students have difficulty taking tests at a computer terminal. Some of this anxiety can be related to lack of computer experience. In preparation for computerized tests, ask the instructor questions about how the test will be structured. Also, make sure you use any opportunities to take practice tests at a learning center or lab.

For some students test anxiety is discipline-specific. For example, some students only have math test anxiety. It is important to distinguish the anxiety that arises from the subject matter itself from more generalized test anxiety. If you need help in thinking through that important distinction, a learning skills specialist or professional counselor can assist you.

Write • DISCUSS • Compare • Ask • BLOG • Answer • *Journal*

Blog about the kinds of situations in which you're most likely to experience test anxiety. Are you more anxious about some types of tests than others, such as tests in particular courses like math or history? Why?

Symptoms of Test Anxiety Test anxiety can manifest itself in many ways, such as butterflies in the stomach, feeling queasy or nauseous, severe headaches, increased heartbeat, hyperventilating, shaking, sweating, or muscle cramps. Students who are overcome by test anxiety can experience the sensation of going blank, unable to remember what they *know* they know. Test anxiety can impede the success of *any* college student, no matter how intelligent, motivated, and prepared. That is why it is critical to seek help from your college or university's counseling service or another professional if you think your test anxiety is affecting your academic performance. A number of simple strategies can help reduce text anxiety. First, any time you begin to feel nervous or upset, take several long deep breaths to restore your breathing to a normal level. This is the quickest and easiest relaxation device.

Other anxiety-reducing techniques include progressive muscle relaxation and visualization. One method of visualization is to create your own peaceful scene and, using all your senses, take yourself there mentally whenever you need to relax.

Tips for Successful Test Taking

The following tips apply to any test situation:

1. **Analyze, ask, and stay calm.** Take a long, deep breath and slowly exhale before you begin. Read all the directions so that you understand what to do. Ask the instructor or exam monitor for clarification if you don't understand something. Be confident. Don't panic. Answer one question at a time.

2. **Make the best use of your time.** Quickly survey the entire test and decide how much time you will spend on each section. Be aware of the point values of different sections of the test. Are some questions worth more points than others?

3. **Answer the easy questions first.** Expect that you'll be puzzled by some questions. Make a note to come back to them later. If different sections consist of different types of questions (such as multiple choice, short answer, and essay), complete the types of question you are most comfortable with first. Be sure to leave enough time for any essays.

4. **If you feel yourself starting to panic or go blank, stop whatever you are doing.** Take a long, deep breath and slowly exhale. Remind yourself you will be OK, that you do know your stuff, and can do well on this test. Then take another deep breath. If necessary, go to another section of the test and come back later to the item that triggered your anxiety.

5. **If you finish early, don't leave.** Stay and check your work for errors. Reread the directions one last time. If using a Scantron answer sheet, make sure that all answers are bubbled accurately and completely.

Essay Questions Many college instructors have a strong preference for the essay exam, for a simple reason: It promotes higher-order critical thinking, whereas other types of exams tend to be exercises in memorization. Generally, the closer you are to graduation, the more essay exams you'll take. To be successful on essay exams, follow these guidelines:

1. **Budget your exam time.** Quickly survey the entire exam, and note the questions that are the easiest for you, along with their point values. Take a moment to weigh their values, and estimate the approximate time you should allot to each question,

Confessions of a College Student

Name: Renée L. Barner

Age: 27

College: Salem Community College

Hometown: Pennsville, New Jersey

Major: Nursing

Favorite book: Anything

Favorite food: Chinese food

Favorite college course: All sciences

The person who inspires me the most or whom I would most like to meet: My mother, who has been the best mother a person could ever want. We did not have a lot of money growing up, but my mother always made sure that we kids were taken care of. We always did fun things together as a family, and she always made us feel that we could reach for the stars as long as we gave our all. She is a wonderful mother, grandmother, and friend.

Heroes: Superman!!!

Favorite way to relax: Watch a movie with my family.

Are you the first to go to college in your family? Yes. Everyone is very proud of me, which has helped me push even harder to achieve.

Test-taking confession: Whenever I study for a test, I always read the material first. I then rewrite my notes and organize them. Then I make flash cards from the notes. If some notes are too long for flash cards, I carefully organize those on a separate sheet of paper. I always use mnemonic devices to help me remember. I make up fake tests and quiz myself on them. I have a friend review the flash cards with me and reread anything that still is not clear to me. Most of the time, it works very well!

and write the time beside each item number. Be sure you know whether you must answer all the questions or choose among questions. Remember, it can be a costly error to write profusely on easy questions of low value, taking up precious time you may need for more important questions. Wear a watch so you can monitor your time, including time at the end for a quick review.

2. **Develop a very brief outline of your answer before you begin to write.** Start working on the questions that are easiest for you, and jot down a few ideas before you begin to write. First, make sure your outline responds to all parts of the question. Then use your first paragraph to introduce the main points and subsequent paragraphs to describe each point in more depth. If you begin to lose your concentration, you will be glad to have the outline to help you regain your focus. If you find that you are running out of time and cannot complete an essay, at the very least provide an outline of key ideas. Instructors usually assign points based on your coverage of the main topics from the material. Thus, you will usually earn more points by responding to all parts of the question briefly than by addressing just one aspect of the question in detail.

3. **Write concise, organized answers.** Because they did not read a question carefully or respond to all parts of a question, many well-prepared students write good answers to questions that were not actually asked. Others hastily write down everything they know on a topic. Answers that are vague and tend to ramble are likely to be downgraded by instructors.

4. Know the key task words in essay questions. Being familiar with the *key word* in an essay question will help you answer it more specifically. The following key task words appear frequently on essay tests. Take time to learn them, so you can answer essay questions more accurately and precisely.

Analyze To divide a subject into its parts in order to understand it better. To show how the parts work together to produce the overall pattern.

Compare To look at the characteristics or qualities of several things and identify their similarities or differences. Do not just describe the traits; define how the things are alike and how they are different.

Contrast To identify the differences between things.

Criticize/Critique To analyze and judge something. Criticism can be positive, negative, or both. A criticism contains your own judgments (supported by evidence) and those of authorities who can support your point.

Define To give the meaning of a word or expression. Giving an example sometimes helps to clarify a definition, although an example by itself is not a definition.

Describe To give a general verbal sketch of something, in narrative or other form.

Discuss To examine or analyze something in a broad and detailed way. Discussion often includes identifying important questions related to an issue and attempting to answer these questions. A good discussion explores all relevant evidence and information.

Evaluate To discuss the strengths and weaknesses of something. Evaluation is similar to criticism, but the word *evaluate* places more stress on how well something meets a certain standard or fulfills some specific purpose.

Explain To clarify something. Explanations generally focus on why or how something has come about.

Interpret To explain the meaning of something. In science, you might explain what an experiment shows and what conclusions can be drawn from it. In a literature course, you might explain—or interpret—what a poem means beyond the literal meaning of the words.

Justify To argue in support of some decision or conclusion by showing sufficient evidence or reasons in its favor. Try to support your argument with logical concrete examples.

Narrate To relate a series of events in the order in which they occurred. Generally, you will also be asked to explain something about the events you are narrating.

Outline To present a series of main points in appropriate order. Some instructors want an outline with Roman numerals for main points followed by letters for supporting details. If in doubt, clarify whether the instructor wants a formal outline.

Prove To give a convincing logical argument and evidence in support of some statement.

Review To summarize and comment on the main parts of a problem or a series of statements. A review question usually also asks you to evaluate or criticize.

Summarize To give information in brief form, omitting examples and details. A summary is short yet covers all important points.

Trace To narrate a course of events. Where possible, you should show connections from one event to the next.

Multiple-Choice Questions Preparing for a multiple-choice test requires you to actively review all of the material that will be covered. Reciting from flash cards, summary sheets, mind maps, or the recall column in your lecture notes is a good way to review such large amounts of information.

Take advantage of the many cues that multiple-choice questions contain. Careful reading of each item can uncover the correct answer. Always question choices that use absolute words such as *always, never,* and *only.* These choices are often (but not always) incorrect. Also, read carefully for terms such as *not, except,* and *but* that are introduced before the choices. Often the answer that is the most inclusive is correct. Generally, options that do not agree grammatically with the first part of the item are incorrect, but this is not always the case.

Some students are easily confused by multiple-choice answers that sound alike. The best way to respond to a multiple-choice question is to read the first part of the item and then predict your own answer before reading the options. Choose the letter that corresponds with the option that best matches your prediction.

If you are totally confused by a question, leave it and come back later, but always double-check that you are filling in the answer for the right question. Sometimes another question will provide a clue for a question you are unsure about. If you have absolutely no idea, look for an answer that at least contains some shred of information. If there is no penalty for guessing, fill in an answer for every question, even if it is just a guess.

Fill-in-the-Blank Questions In many ways preparing for fill-in-the-blank questions is similar to getting ready for multiple-choice items, but fill-in-the-blank is harder because you do not have a choice of possible answers right in front of you. Not all fill-in-the-blank questions are constructed the same way. Some instructors will provide a series of blanks to give you a clue regarding the number of words in the answer, but if just one long blank is provided you cannot assume that the answer is just one word. If possible, ask the instructor whether the answer is supposed to be a single word per blank or can be a longer phrase.

True/False Questions Remember, for the question to be true, every detail of the question must be true. Questions containing words such as *always, never,* and *only* are usually false, whereas less definite terms such as *often* and *frequently* suggest the statement may be true. Read through the entire exam to see whether information in one question can help you answer another. Do not begin to second-guess what you know or doubt your answers because a sequence of questions appears to be all true or all false.

Matching Questions The matching question is the hardest to answer by guessing. In one column you will find the term, in the other the description of it. Before answering any question, review all of the terms and descriptions. Match those terms you are sure of first. As you do so, cross out both the term and its description, and then use the process of elimination to assist you in answering the remaining items. Flash cards and lists that can be created from the recall column in your notes are excellent ways to prepare for matching questions.

WIRED WINDOW

EVEN IF YOU ARE typically enrolled in traditional face-to-face courses, you will undoubtedly take an increasing number of your exams online through course management systems (like eCollege and Blackboard). Some of the same tips for successful test taking also apply to online exams. Ensure that you will be in a quiet area free of distractions while you take the exam. Learn about constraints (e.g., time limit, due date) before the exam by asking your professor or logging in early to see whether the constraints are posted online. If you haven't already done so, take a practice test so that you are familiar with the online testing interface. If there is no time limit, take a break after you complete the exam and then go back and recheck your answers. If there is a time limit and the course management system does not show a timer, use a stopwatch or countdown timer to track your progress. (A good rule of thumb is to have the countdown timer sound once, with enough time left for you to review the entire exam and then review again with five minutes left.) Since you won't have a paper exam, you'll be unable to take notes on the exam itself. Be prepared to have a notepad with you to jot down notes. You also won't be able to easily move back and forth between the pages of the exam to review your answers or skip questions for later. Therefore, when reviewing your answers or going back to previous questions, make sure that you have saved every page of the exam. If you save your exam and have not yet submitted it for grading, you can use your browser's back button to review questions and answers on previous pages.

Write • DISCUSS • Compare • Ask • BLOG • Answer • *Journal*

Which kinds of test questions (for example, multiple-choice, matching, true/false, fill in the blank, essay) tend to be the most difficult for you? The easiest? Why?

Types of Tests

Problem-Solving Tests In the physical and biological sciences, mathematics, engineering, statistics, and symbolic logic, some tests will require you to solve problems showing *all* steps. Even if you know a shortcut, it is important to document how you got from step A to step B. On other tests all that will matter is whether you have the correct solution to the problem, although doing all the steps will still help ensure you get the right answer. For these tests you must also be very careful that you have made no errors in your scientific notation. A misplaced sign, parenthesis, bracket, or exponent can make all the difference.

Be sure that you read all directions carefully. Are you required to reduce the answer to simplest terms? Are you supposed to graph the solution? Be careful when canceling terms, cross multiplying, distributing terms, and combining fractions. Whenever possible, after you complete the problem work it backwards to check your solution, or plug your solution back into the equation to make sure it adds up. Also check to make sure your solution makes sense. You cannot have negative bushels of apples, for example, a fraction of a person, or a correlation less than negative 1 or greater than 1.

Machine-Scored Tests It is important to follow the directions for machine-scored tests carefully. Be sure that in addition to your name you provide all the information sought on the answer sheet, such as the instructor's name, the number for the class section, and your student ID number. Each time you fill in an answer, make sure the number on the answer sheet corresponds with the number of the item on the test. If you have questions that you want to come back to, mark them on the test itself (if you are allowed to do so) rather than on the answer sheet.

Although scoring machines have become more sophisticated over time, stray marks on your answer sheet can still be misread and throw off the scoring. When a machine-scored test is returned to you, check your answer sheet against the scoring key, if provided, to make sure you received credit for all questions you answered correctly.

Computerized Tests Your comfort with taking computerized tests can depend on how computer-literate you are in general for objective tests as well as your keyboarding skills for essay exams. If your instructor provides an opportunity for practice tests, be sure to take advantage of this chance to get a better sense of how the tests will be structured. There can be significant variations depending on the kind of test, the academic subject, and whether the test was constructed by the instructor or by a textbook company or other source.

For multiple-choice and other objective forms of computerized tests, you may be allowed to scroll down and back through the entire test, but this is not always the case. Sometimes you are only allowed to see one question at a time and after you complete that question you are not be allowed to go back to it. In this situation you cannot skip questions that are hard and come back to them later, so be sure you try to answer every question.

For computerized tests in math and other subjects that require you to solve each problem, record an answer and then move to the next problem. Be sure to check each answer before you submit it. Also know in advance which materials you are allowed to have on hand and whether these include a calculator and scratch paper for working the problems.

Laboratory Tests In many science courses and in some other academic disciplines, you will be required to take lab tests, during which you rotate from one lab station to the next to solve problems, identify parts of models or specimens, explain chemical reactions, and complete other tasks similar to those you have been performing in a lab. At some colleges and universities, lab tests are now administered at computer terminals via simulations. To prepare for lab tests, always attend lab; take good notes, including diagrams and other visual representations as necessary; and be sure to study your lab notebook carefully prior to the test. If possible, create your own diagrams or models, and then see whether you can label them without looking at your book.

You may also have to take lab tests in foreign language courses. These tests can have both oral and written components. Work with a partner or study group to prepare for oral exams. Ask one another questions that require using key vocabulary words. Try recording your answers to work on your pronunciation.

Particularly in foreign languages that use a different symbol system, such as Chinese, you may also have computerized lab tests that require you to identify syllables or words and indicate the order and direction of the strokes required to create them. The best way to prepare for these tests is to learn the meaning and parts of the symbols and practice writing them regularly.

Open-Book and Open-Notes Tests If you never had open-book or open-notes tests in high school, you may be tempted to study less thoroughly, thinking you will have access to all the information you need during the test. This is a common misjudgment on the part of first-year students. Open-book and open-notes tests are usually *harder* than other exams, not easier.

Most students do not really have time to spend looking up things during this type of exam. The best way to prepare is to begin the same way you would study for a test in which you cannot refer to your notes or text. But as you do so, develop a list of topics and the page numbers where they are covered in your text. You may want to use the same strategy in organizing your lecture notes. Number the pages in your notebook. Later type a three-column grid (or use an Excel spreadsheet) with your list of topics in alphabetical order in the first column and corresponding pages from your text and notebook in the second and third columns so that you can refer to them quickly if necessary. Or you may want to paste colored tabs on your textbook or notebook pages for different topics. But whatever you do, study as completely as you would for any other test, and do not be fooled into thinking that you do not need to know the material thoroughly.

During the test, monitor your time carefully. Do not waste time unnecessarily looking up information in your text or notes to double-check yourself if you are confident of your answers. Instead, wait until you have finished the test, and then, if you have extra time, go back and look up answers and make any necessary changes. But if you have really studied, you probably will not find this necessary.

Sometimes the only reason an instructor allows open books or open notes is so students can properly reference their sources when responding to essay or short-answer tests. Make sure you are aware whether you are expected to document your answers and provide a reference or works cited list.

Take-Home Tests Like open-book and open-notes tests, take-home tests are usually more difficult than in-class tests and are almost always essay tests. Be sure to allow plenty of time to complete a take-home test. Read the directions and questions as soon as you receive the test in order to gauge how much time you will need. If the test is all essays, consider how much time you might allocate to writing several papers of the same length. Remember, your instructor will expect your essay answers to look more like assigned out-of-class papers than like the essays you would write during an in-class test.

Unfortunately, academic honesty issues can arise for take-home tests. If you are accustomed to working with a study group for the course or in a learning community, check with the instructor in advance to determine the extent to which collaboration is allowed on the take-home test. One situation that can be very confusing for students is to have been encouraged to work together throughout the academic term, only to be told there should be no communication outside of class on a take-home test.

Academic Honesty

Imagine where society would be if researchers reported fraudulent results that were then used to develop new machines or medical treatments. Integrity is a cornerstone of higher education, and activities that compromise that integrity damage everyone: your country, your community, your college or university, your classmates, and yourself.

Types of Misconduct

Institutions vary widely in how they define broad terms such as *lying* or *cheating*. Generally, cheating is defined as using or trying to use unauthorized notes, materials, or other devices during a test or when preparing an assignment. This would apply to looking over a classmate's shoulder for an answer, using a calculator when it is not authorized, procuring or discussing an exam (or individual questions from an exam) without permission, copying lab notes, purchasing term papers over the Internet, watching the video instead of reading the book, and duplicating computer files. Plagiarism, or taking another person's ideas or work and presenting them as your own, is especially intolerable in academic culture. Just as taking someone else's property constitutes physical theft, taking credit for someone else's ideas constitutes intellectual theft.

On most tests, you do not have to credit specific individuals. (But some instructors do require this; when in doubt, ask!) In written reports and papers, however, you must give credit any time you use (a) another person's actual words, (b) another person's ideas or theories—even if you don't quote them directly, and (c) any other information not considered common knowledge.

Many schools prohibit other activities besides lying, cheating, unauthorized assistance, and plagiarism. Examples of prohibited behaviors include intentionally inventing information or results, earning credit more than once for the same piece of academic work without permission, giving your work or exam answers to another student to copy during an actual exam or before an exam is given to another section, and bribing in exchange for any kind of academic advantage. Most schools also outlaw helping or attempting to help another student commit a dishonest act.

Write • DISCUSS • Compare • Ask • BLOG • Answer • *Journal*

> Think about one occasion when you saw a student you know cheating. How did that incident make you feel about that student, the circumstances, and yourself?

WHERE TO GO FOR HELP

On Campus

Learning Assistance Support Center Almost every campus has one of these, and helping students study for tests is one of their specialties. The best students, good students who want to be the best students, and students with academic difficulties use learning centers and tutoring services. These services are offered by both full-time professionals and highly skilled student tutors.

Counseling Services College and university counseling centers offer a wide array of services, often including workshops and individual or group counseling for test anxiety. Sometimes these services are also offered by the campus health center.

Fellow College Students Often the best help you can get is the closest. Keep an eye out in your classes, residence hall, extracurricular activities, and so forth for the best students, those who appear to be the most serious, purposeful, and directed. Hire a tutor. Join a study group.

Online

Read the following two websites. Take notes.

Write a summary of what you believe to be the important facts.

The Academic Center for Excellence, University of Illinois at Chicago: http://www.uic.edu/depts/counselctr/ace/examprep.htm.

Learning Centre of the University of New South Wales in Sydney, Australia: http://www.lc.unsw.edu.au/onlib/exam.html.

Developing Values

In this chapter YOU WILL LEARN

▶ How to define *values*

▶ Distinctions between types of values

▶ How societal values are in conflict

▶ How changes in American society have forced changes in societal values

▶ How to put values to the test through service learning

© AP Photo/Mel Evans

John M. Whiteley and James B. Craig of the University of California-Irvine and Edward Zlotkowski of Bentley College contributed their valuable and considerable expertise to the writing of this chapter.

How Do You DEVELOP YOUR VALUES?

Read the following questions and choose the answer that fits you best.

1 *How would you define the word* values?

(A) It means the things a person thinks are important like a car or a boat.

(B) It means the way you think about certain issues like drinking alcohol or having sex before you are married.

(C) The word *values* is a really broad term that has many different meanings.

2 *What do you do when your values are in conflict with your friends' values?*

(A) I tell them how they should think and act. It's my responsibility to change them.

(B) I may try to change them, but after awhile I give up and find new friends.

(C) I try to understand their point of view if I disagree with them. If we continue talking to each other, we're more likely to appreciate each other's position.

3 *Do you think college students should take part in service activities in the local community?*

(A) No. I think college students should spend their time learning from their professors and participating in campus activities.

(B) It depends on the activity. There are some situations that would scare me, and I wouldn't want to go to a really bad neighborhood.

(C) I think community service is a way to expand learning. It's an important part of a college education.

4 *Do you think that colleges and universities should have honor codes?*

(A) I don't think anyone pays attention to these, so writing them is a waste of time.

(B) Maybe church-related colleges should have these, but not public institutions.

(C) I think all colleges need some sort of broad statement about the way students should act on campus. I'm going to find my campus's honor code and read it.

Review your responses. (A) responses indicate that you haven't really thought much about the topic of values. (B) responses indicate that you're spent some time clarifying your values, but you'll definitely benefit from more information. (C) responses indicate that you've thought a great deal about your values and how they are important in the college environment. Whatever your responses, you will find this chapter provides information that will help you understand the roles of values on campus and in the world beyond.

The word *values* means different things to different people. For some, the word refers to specific views a person holds on controversial moral issues, such as capital punishment. For others, it refers to whatever is most important to a person, such as a good job, a fancy car, or the welfare of one's family. For still others, it refers to abstract concepts such as truth, justice, or success.

In this chapter, we offer definitions of values, provide a framework for thinking about values, and explore ways for you to discover your values and apply them not only to the college experience but also to life after college.

Defining Values

Perhaps we can best define a value as an important attitude or belief that commits a person to take action, to do something. For instance, you might watch a television program showing the devastation caused by the May 2008 earthquake in China and feel sympathy or regret without taking any action whatsoever. If your feelings of sympathy cause you to take action to help others, those feelings qualify as values.

Actions do not have to be overtly physical. They can involve thinking and talking continually about a problem, trying to interest others in it, reading about it, or sending letters to officials regarding it. The basic point is that when someone truly holds a value, it leads that person to do something.

We can also define values as beliefs that people accept by choice, with a sense of responsibility and ownership. Much of what people think is simply what others have taught them. Many things people have learned from their parents and others close to them will count as their values, but only after they fully embrace these values themselves. You must personally accept or reject something before it can become a value for you.

Finally, the idea of *affirmation*, or *prizing*, is an essential part of values. When you affirm and prize your values, you proudly declare them to be true, readily accept the choices to which they lead, and want others to know them. You also find yourself ready to sacrifice for them and to establish your priorities around them. Your values govern your loyalties and commitments.

In summary, then, values are those important attitudes or beliefs that people (1) accept by choice, (2) affirm with pride, and (3) express in action.

In contemporary society, many basic institutions put pressure on you to choose what they believe are the "correct" values when in fact those values are often in conflict with your own. It is important for you to recognize your own values, even though they may differ from those around you.

Every one of us has felt some well-intentioned pressures from family and friends to make the "right" value choices. But within a democratic free society, a basic human right is to choose your own values. This chapter will empower you to understand more about the origins and forms of pressure on you to make particular value choices and will help you define your uniqueness.

Scholars have classified values in different ways, and it is essential to understand those different classifications. The nature of the human condition is that people are like each other in many ways, but special characteristics make each person unique. How you choose to establish values different from those of your friends, your family, your society, and its institutions is what helps you become distinctive.

Write • DISCUSS • Compare • Ask • BLOG • Answer • *Journal*

Do you and your friends have the same or different values? How do you know? How does having the same values impact your friendships? How does having different values impact your relationships?

Types of Values

There are a number of useful ways of thinking about values in practice. One approach is to distinguish among *moral values*, *aesthetic values*, and *performance values*. Another is to consider *ends* versus *means* values.

Moral Values **Moral values** are those personal values that you generally do not attempt to force on others but that are of immense importance to you as an individual, such as, "I believe it is wrong to lie because lying shows disrespect for other people." These moral values are used to justify your own behavior toward others (as well as to privately judge others). New college students may find that as family and peer group influence diminishes, the college years represent a significant opportunity to focus, often for the first time, on the choice of moral values to live by.

Aesthetic Values **Aesthetic values** are the standards by which people judge beauty. Beauty, as used here, refers to a broad set of judgments about nature, art, music, literature, personal appearance, and so on. For example, people make different value judgments about music, about what is of value artistically, and about which types of books are worth reading. Within society, vast differences of opinion exist about the definition of proper aesthetic values and how to judge beauty—and even about what beauty is.

Performance Values There is comparatively less difference of opinion about nonmoral **performance values**, or how well a person performs according to some standard, at least within most campus and other institutional cultures. The definition of performance can vary from person to person or context to context, but representative performance values are accuracy, speed, accomplishment, reward, and discipline. These performance values can have a moral component when judgments are made about specific individuals or groups of people with similar characteristics concerning how they measure up to some performance standard.

Performance values influence college students through the expectations of them held by important people in their lives such as parents and instructors.

Means Values versus Ends Values Values can also be classified as *means values* or *ends values.* Ends, or *intrinsic*, values refer to ultimate goals such as a world at peace, a comfortable life, freedom, wisdom, and true friendship. Means, or *instrumental*, values are values that are used to help one attain other values such as being responsible, obedient, loving, imaginative, ambitious, independent, or honest.

When you think about your values, you should realize that they do not always separate clearly into means and ends categories. The fundamental American value of equality of opportunity, for example, is frequently offered as an intrinsic value of U.S. society and one of the values that distinguishes the United States from totalitarian countries. But equality of opportunity can also be instrumental in the achievement of other intrinsic values such as the enhancement of human dignity, the realization of human potential, and the liberation of the human spirit, which puts it in the category of a means value.

Challenges to Personal Values in College

Most students find that college life challenges their existing personal and moral values. New students are often startled at the diversity of personal moralities found on campus. For instance, you may have been taught that it is wrong to drink alcohol, yet you find that friends whom you respect and care about see nothing wrong with drinking. At the same time, students from more liberal backgrounds may be astonished to discover themselves forming friendships with classmates whose personal values are very conservative.

Write • DISCUSS • Compare • Ask • BLOG • Answer • *Journal*

> Have any of your values changed since you have been in college? Where do you see yourself in terms of your values at this point in your college career?

When you don't approve of aspects of a friend's way of life, do you try to change his or her behavior, pass judgment on the person, or withdraw from the relationship? Often, part of the problem is that the friend demonstrates countless good qualities and values that make the troublesome conduct seem less significant. In the process, your own values may begin to change under the influence of a new kind of relativism: "I don't choose to do that, but I'm not going to make any judgments against those who do." In cases when a friendship is affected by differing values, tolerance is generally a good goal.

Tolerance for others is a central value in American society and one that often grows during college. Even so, it is easy to think of cases in which tolerance gradually becomes an indulgence of another's destructive tendencies. It is one thing to accept a friend's responsible use of alcohol at a party and quite another to fail to challenge a drunk who plans to drive you home. Sexual intimacy in an enduring relationship is

Confessions of a College Student

Name: Molly Reese

Age: 20

University: New York University, Gallatin School of Individualized Study

Hometown: Hanover, Massachusetts

Major: Individualized French, Italian, Comparative Literature

Favorite book(s): *Out of Africa*

Favorite college course: It's a tie between "Intro. to Comparative Literature: Promiscuous Readers/Worldy Texts" and "Translation" (French/English)

The person who inspires me the most or whom I would most like to meet: Henry David Thoreau. I think we would have been friends! And I would love to have been able to see what he was like in day-to-day life.

Heroes: Karen Blixen (a.k.a. Isak Dinesen) of *Out of Africa* and M.F.K. Fisher—they were both strong, independent women during times when such a thing was rare. They were also very passionate people, which I admire because their lives seemed to be fulfilled by these passions. I also admire them because they found pleasure not only in the grand adventures they had but also in simple things.

Favorite way to relax: I love reading and drinking coffee.

Your proudest moment or biggest accomplishment: Completing a semester abroad in France during high school and learning French.

Favorite food: Steak

My values confession: I would say that the values most important to me are acceptance, sincerity, and diligence. I feel like I learned/developed what values I have from a variety of sources—parents, friends, friends' parents, and literature. I've always been inspired to do "the right thing" so that my parents and the people who instilled values in me would be proud. I think I learned most of these values by example. My parents were never very heavy-handed with proverbs or "lessons" but surrounded my brother and me (and themselves) with people whose values they admired. None of these people was perfect or saintly, but most of them were open about their mistakes. I have definitely struggled with my values, especially once I got to college and was far enough away from my parents that they might not find out about what I was doing. I remember wanting to go home for Christmas break early and wanting to lie to a professor about having to go home for a family emergency so I could take the final earlier. My roommate convinced me not to—but I would like to think I wouldn't have gone through with it even if she hadn't talked to me. When I have what I think to be a morally challenging decision to make, I find that if I just let it sit and think about it long enough without acting, the right thing to do or to say will come to me, but I tend to be a bit impatient, so sometimes this is hard. That's when I go back to not wanting to disappoint earnest people. Since I have gone to college, not only have I sometimes struggled to stick to my values, but some of my values have changed or evolved. I value sincerity more than ever, and I think this is because most people come face-to-face with much more difficult problems in college, and I think that sincerity is paramount to handling these sorts of situations. My appreciation for acceptance of others also grew because of the diverse (in every respect) group of people I met at college.

one thing; a never-ending series of one-night stands is quite another. Remember, the failure to challenge destructive conduct is no sign of friendship.

Your challenge is to balance your personal welfare, your tolerance for diversity, and your freedom of choice. It can be very enriching and rewarding to talk about values with someone whose values seem in conflict with your own.

Each of you can learn a great deal from talking about what you value and why. Many people flee from diversity and fail to confront conflicting value systems when, realistically speaking, the values of our society change over time and many deeply held societal values are in serious conflict. Adopting a set of values that truly makes sense to you can help you move ahead with your life and enable you to consciously analyze and reflect on what is taking place in society.

Societal Values in Conflict: Value Dualisms

Societal values—values held by a society—are often conflicting. And because your values are influenced by the culture in which you live, you can have conflicting values as well. Your conflicting beliefs, or *value dualisms*, which you may or may not have examined, derive from many different life experiences. For instance, you might believe that Americans should conserve fuel yet also believe it is your "right" to drive a gas-guzzling car.

Another common value dualism that provokes different reactions is the issue of poverty. Some people believe strongly that poverty should be abolished by government action, while others believe that some people will always be poor because they don't work hard enough.

Apply this dualism to a contemporary problem in American society. According to the U. S. Census Bureau, in 2006 about 36.5 million U.S. citizens were living below the official poverty level, and almost 13 million of those citizens were under the age of 18. Given the immense wealth of the United States, to allow large numbers of individuals, especially children and adolescents, to subsist in poverty is simply not a rational choice. Yet we are not able to reach a consensus on how to solve this problem.

Changing Society, Changing Values

Changes in society dramatically affect not only the values of society but also of individuals. As new knowledge and new technologies change the world around you, your values are challenged. Consider recent changes in some of the fundamental institutions of American society, including family, religion, education, and the position of the United States in the global marketplace. Also think about stem cell research, cloning, and the ability of medical science to keep people alive far beyond their ability to survive on their own. These new frontiers of knowledge create challenges to the values held by society and by individuals.

If values did not (or could not) change with the changing society, people would never make progress. At the same time, it is all the more difficult to define and hold to enduring values.

WIRED WINDOW

WHETHER YOU KNOW it or not, you are making statements about your values all the time. One place where you express your values, possibly without even knowing you are doing so, is through your profile on social networking sites like Facebook and MySpace. Information on your profile communicates your likes, dislikes, and values toward various issues. For instance, a quote that you have posted on your profile can reflect a value even if it doesn't directly assert that value. When posting a quote, you are implicitly declaring your agreement with the author (who, more than likely, was communicating a personal value through the statement). As an exercise in examining your values, pretend that you are someone who doesn't know you and is reading one of your profile pages for the first time. What would this stranger think about you and what you value? Which *moral values* are you expressing on your page? If you can't tell right away, think about whether you list your religious preference. What does that communicate to others? Think about your choice of music—does the music you enjoy communicate something about your *aesthetic values*? What *societal values* are you expressing by simply having a page on a social networking site? What about those who choose not to have a profile page? What values might they be expressing through their choice?

The traditional family of earlier generations does not serve as a model for society today. Many more women are working outside the home than was the case fifty years ago. As of 2006, according to the U.S. Department of Labor, 56 percent of women over age sixteen were working. But many women still retain responsibility for the lion's share of household duties while also experiencing discrimination in the workplace.

If continuing changes in society are affecting values within families, what are the implications for today's college students? What do we mean by a "generation gap" between this generation of college students and the generation of their parents? As roles of men and women within families continue to change, how does someone in college decide which enduring values work for him or her? What enduring values should you seek in a significant other? These are important questions you should explore in college and beyond.

Service Learning and Values

One of the most effective ways to explore values is through a concept that is anything but abstract: *service learning.*

Service Learning Defined

Service learning is a teaching method that combines meaningful service to the community with curriculum-based learning.

▶ **Serving.** The service itself should address a *genuine community need*, as determined by existing or student-led community assessments. The service should be thoughtfully organized to solve, or make a positive contribution toward solving, a problem.

▶ **Linking.** In quality service learning, the service project is designed to meet not only a real community need but also *classroom goals*. By ensuring strong linkages between service and learning, you can improve your academic skills, applying what you learn in school to the broader community and what you learn from community involvement to your academic work.

▶ **Learning.** *Reflection* is a key element of service learning. The instructor structures time and methods for students to reflect on their service experience.

In other words, service learning is both related to and yet different from two kinds of off-campus activity with which you are probably familiar: community service and internships. Like community service, service learning seeks to help others and to contribute to the common good. Indeed, students involved in service learning and in community service often work at the same community site.

But there are also important differences, such as service learning's emphasis on *reflection* (careful thought, especially the process of reconsidering previous actions, events, or decisions) and *reciprocity* (something done mutually or in return). Although a student *can* learn a lot through traditional community service, service learning does not leave such learning to chance.

Instead it surrounds the service experience with carefully designed opportunities for reflection to help students prepare for, process, and pull together different aspects of their experience. Because reflection and reciprocity require some kind of formal structure to make them effective, service learning takes place in specially designed academic courses. Let us look at some reasons more and more students are making service learning an important part of their education.

Using Service Learning to Clarify Values

There is probably no better way for people to clarify what they really value than to put themselves in situations in which their assumptions and beliefs are tested. Suppose you've always assumed you wanted to be an accountant. You take a course with a service-learning requirement that asks you to "reconcile the books" at a local nonprofit organization. You set about introducing some logic in their accounting procedures—but you hate the job. Or suppose you've always believed you wanted to be an instructor, and your service-learning assignment is to teach a group of immigrant fourth-grade students how to read in English. You find either that you are able to teach these students effectively or that you simply don't have the patience such a job requires. In either case you learn that your untested beliefs about what you value in a work situation are challenged by reality. And as a result of your experience, you now have some important additional information with which to make your career choice.

Identifying Value Dualisms

Earlier in this chapter we discussed value dualisms—explicit (or, more often, implicit) conflicts between a person's different beliefs. Service learning is one of the most powerful tools you have to bring such conflicts to consciousness. In other words, it helps you better understand your personal value system and the strength of your professed beliefs.

Although most students find the very experience of being on campus a good opportunity to re-examine personal values, it's also true that most people quickly seek out others more or less similar to themselves. Service learning helps to ensure that your college years really do teach you to stretch and to move outside your comfort zone.

Developing Skills

Still another set of benefits associated with service learning has to do with skills and competencies. You know you'll need to be able to think on your feet once you graduate. But how do you learn to do that in a course in which the instructor frames all the problems and does most of the talking? You'd also like to improve your public speaking skills, but will in-class presentations provide you with the practice you need? And what about writing, time management, and intercultural communication—not just for your classes but for the world beyond? For many students, service learning means knowing not just *about* things but *how to do* them. It juxtaposes theories and ideas with concrete personal experience and in doing so helps students learn how to act on their knowledge and put theory to the test. Hence it is an especially effective way to develop critical-thinking skills.

Civic Engagement

Civic engagement is participation in activities to improve your community, region, or the nation. For instance, working to register new voters is a form of civic engagement.

In February 2003 a group of Oklahoma students issued what they called a "Civic Engagement Resolution." In it they complained that "higher education institutions do not provide adequate education and knowledge about our civic responsibilities. We often do not know how to address civic issues. Higher education's primary focus is to produce professionals, when instead they should be producing citizens." Although it has become common to criticize the younger generation as politically apathetic, surveys indicate that more young people today are engaged in community service than at any time in the past. Yet they are given little guidance on how to develop their service activity into genuine civic engagement.

As the Oklahoma students point out, higher education certainly is not doing its part. Service learning speaks directly to this problem. Indeed, facilitating civic engagement is one of its most important benefits.

Service learning is one of the very few teaching-learning strategies that provides an equal opportunity to succeed for all kinds of learners—not only students who learn well from books and who are perceptive listeners but also students who learn best through active experimentation and hands-on projects. Service learning directly addresses a question often on the tip of a student's tongue: Why do I have to learn this? Because service-learning experiences let students see the utility of their knowledge even as they develop it, those experiences tend to stand out as especially meaningful—and transformative.

Values and You

With all of this in mind, what kinds of values do you and other college students believe should characterize a society in which you soon will play a leadership role? Does your generation of college students want to unravel some of the value dualisms discussed in this chapter? If you were to revisit some of the same issues fifty years from now, what social values would you like to see more fully actualized in practice? What dominant social values do you want to pass on to your children? College offers a time to reflect on the purpose of learning and on the uses to which you will put your knowledge. Values are a central element in this reflection.

College is also a time to reflect on the ethical dilemmas that confront citizens individually and as members of society. An essential goal of a college education is to cultivate a capacity for reflection about, and analysis of, values issues in society and in one's personal life.

A preparation for life as well as for a career, college is an opportunity for personal development, including—quite centrally—values development. It is vitally important to learn to integrate both intellectual development and personal value development.

▷ Where To Go For **HELP**

On Campus

Counselors, chaplains, academic advisors, and your own *college instructors* are all great resources for helping you sort out and think through the challenges you face in dealing with values in college—both your own and those of others around you. In fact, anyone who has come to know you could be a person you can converse with on this critical topic of growth and change during college. The most important thing is to reflect on this topic and then talk about it with others.

Online

Journal of College and Character http://www. collegevalues.org/reflections.cfm. Check out this website to learn how you can contribute an essay on values to this journal published at Florida State University, and read essays written by other college students from around the United States.

Information about Campus Honor Codes http:// www.academicintegrity.org/codes_and_policies/index.php. Many college and university campuses in the United States have honor codes. See this website to compare and contrast campus expectations of students' moral and ethical behavior.

The University of South Carolina's "Carolinian Creed" http://www.sa.sc.edu/CREED/. This is one example of how a large university chooses to state its core values.

Diversity: Appreciating Differences Among Us

CHAPTER 11

In this chapter YOU WILL LEARN

▶ The concepts of culture, diversity, ethnicity, and multiculturalism

▶ The value of gaining knowledge of various ethnic and cultural groups

▶ The role colleges play in promoting diversity

▶ How to identify and cope with discrimination and prejudice on campus

© Blend Images/SuperStock

Juan J. Flores of Folsom Lake College contributed his valuable and considerable expertise to the writing of this chapter.

How Do You APPRECIATE DIVERSITY?

A?B?C?A?B?C?A?B?C?

Read the following questions and choose the answer that most fits you:

1 What terms do you associate with diversity?

A I think diversity just means differences among things or people. You can divide people into any kinds of categories you can think up.

B *Culture* is the only term I can think of.

C Some words like *race* and *ethnicity* come to mind, but there must be others.

2 Do you consider yourself open to differing values and beliefs?

A I think I am quite tolerant of others' beliefs and our differences—it's an opportunity to learn something new from someone else.

B I haven't been exposed to many people different from myself, so it's hard to say.

C I try to be open to people different from myself, but I don't think we have much in common—so I don't have many friends who are different.

3 We all have prejudices and biases. How have you dealt with yours?

A I always keep an open mind and hear people out. I remember that it's OK to have differences of opinion among people, as long as you can respect others' beliefs and not put them down just because they are different from you.

B What's there to deal with? I just stick with people like myself.

C Keeping an open mind is how I try to deal with it, but it doesn't always seem to work.

4 How do you seek out opportunities to learn about cultures and groups other than your own?

A I join various extracurricular groups to explore different viewpoints, beliefs, and people.

B I don't really go outside my comfort zone.

C I tend to stay with my own kind, but I'm sometimes introduced to new cultures and people by my friends, which I always find fun and interesting.

5 How would you react if there were a hate crime at your school?

A I would get involved and do whatever I could to help make the situation better.

B I'd be sorry it happened, but I'd rather not get involved.

C People are people, and these things are going to happen. There's nothing you can do about it.

Review your responses. **A** responses indicate that you are open to meeting diverse people and having diverse experiences. **B** responses indicate that you haven't had much experience with people or ideas out of your comfort zone. **C** responses indicate that although you've had some experience with diversity, it is still hard for you to explore different people and ideas. Whatever your current attitude about or experience with diversity, this chapter will give you new ideas about why diversity is so important and how to go about exploring varied experiences and opportunities while you're in college.

Colleges and universities serve as microcosms of the "real world" ahead—a world that requires people to work, live, and socialize with various ethnic and cultural groups. In few other settings do the multitudes of ethnic and cultural groups interact in such close proximity to one another as they do on a college campus. Whether you are attending a university or community college, you will be exposed to new experiences and opportunities, all of which enhance learning and a deeper sense of understanding.

Through self-assessment, discovery, and open-mindedness, you can begin to understand your perspectives on diversity. This work, although difficult at times, will enhance your educational experiences, personal growth, and development. Thinking critically about your personal values and belief systems allows you to have a greater sense of belonging and make a positive contribution to our multicultural society.

The Importance of Understanding Diversity

Diversity is the variation in social and cultural identity among people living together in a defined setting. As your journey through higher education unfolds, you will find yourself immersed in this mixture of identities. Regardless of the size of the college or university, going to college brings together people of differing backgrounds and experiences but with common goals and aspirations. Each person brings to campus a unique life story, upbringing, value system, view of the world, and set of judgments. You can tap these differences to enhance your experiences in the classes you take, the organizations you join, and the relationships you cultivate. For many students, college is the first time they are exposed to so much diversity. Learning experiences and challenges await you both in and out of the classroom. It's a chance to learn, not only about others, but also about yourself.

Self-reflection and discovery will occasionally require you to consider some tough questions about your views of diversity, biases, and prejudices. Some of these questions may make you a bit uncomfortable. It is safe to say that everyone has some sort of prejudice against a different group or value system. To say otherwise is unrealistic. Yet it is what you do with your individual beliefs that separates you from the racist, the bigot, and the extremist. Being open and honest in answering the self-assessment provides a foundation on which you can build. Armed with your responses, you can begin to uncover how your views developed and whether or not you want to take steps to adjust them.

Ethnicity and Culture

Often the terms *ethnicity* and *culture* are used interchangeably, although in reality their definitions are quite distinct. Throughout this chapter, we will use these two words together and in isolation. Before we start using the terms, it's a good idea to define them so that you know what they actually mean.

Ethnicity refers to a quality assigned to a specific group of people historically connected by a common national origin or language. For example, let's look at one of the largest ethnic groups, Latinos. Latin America encompasses over thirty countries from North America to the Caribbean, all of which share the Spanish language. A notable exception is Brazil. Although the national language is Portuguese, Brazilians are considered Latinos. The countries also share many traditions and beliefs, with some variations. However, we shouldn't generalize with this or any ethnic group. Not every Latino who speaks Spanish is of Mexican descent, and not every Latino speaks Spanish. Acknowledging that differences do exist within ethnic groups is a big step in becoming ethnically aware.

Culture is defined as those aspects of a group of people that are passed on or learned. Traditions, food, language, clothing styles, artistic expression, and beliefs are all part of culture. With this definition in mind, we can begin to rethink the common mistake that assigns culture to only ethnic groups. Certainly ethnic groups are also cultural groups: They share common language, foods, traditions, art, and clothing, which are passed from one generation to the next. But nonethnic cultural groups can fit this concept of culture, too. Think of the hip-hop community. In the hip-hop world there is a common style of dress, specific terminology used in hip-hop circles, and shared musical and artistic expression—all of which can be learned and passed on to others.

Although we don't use the term *race* very often in this chapter, it's important to discuss the idea of race as it is commonly used in everyday language. Race refers to biological characteristics shared by groups of people and includes hair texture and color, skin tone, and facial features. Making generalizations about someone's racial group affiliation is risky. For instance, can we say that an individual with black, tightly woven hair is always of African or African-American descent? Certainly not, since a person of Dominican or Puerto Rican or Cuban descent can have that same black, tightly woven hair texture. Even people who share some biological features—such as similar eye shape or a dark skin—can be ethnically very distinct. For instance, people of Asian descent are not necessarily ethnically and culturally alike, since Asia is a vast region encompassing such disparate places as Mongolia, India, and Japan. Likewise, people of African descent can be from very different backgrounds; the African continent is home to fifty-three countries and hundreds of different languages, and Africans are genetically very diverse.

Making assumptions about group identity based on traits can do more harm than good. It helps to try to become more aware of the variations of ethnicity, culture, and race in society. No one is expecting you to be an expert, now or in the future. In fact, with so much variation within groups themselves, to think you have ethnicity, culture, and race all figured out is fooling yourself. The best approach is to avoid making quick judgments or assigning group labels.

Write • DISCUSS • Compare • Ask • BLOG • Answer • *Journal*

> How do you compare the diversity in your former school or work setting to the diversity you are experiencing at this campus? How is the level of racial or cultural diversity in college different from or similar to your prior experience?

Multiculturalism in Higher Education

Acknowledging the importance of diversity in education, colleges and universities have begun to apply this concept to student learning opportunities. **Multiculturalism** is the active process of acknowledging and respecting the various social groups, cultures, religions, races, ethnicities, attitudes, and opinions within an environment. We see this in efforts by colleges to embrace an *inclusive curriculum.* Today you can find courses with a multicultural focus in various departments of your college or university, many of which have been approved to meet graduation requirements. Numerous colleges and universities have established specific academic departments with majors in gender studies, ethnic and cultural studies, and religious studies, to name a few.

Confessions of a College Student

Name: Daniel R. Anderson

Age: 19

University: University of Delaware

Hometown: West Milford, New Jersey

Major: Psychology

Favorite book: *To Kill A Mockingbird*

Favorite college course: Education 240 (Philosophical and Legal Perspectives). This course reviews Supreme Court cases dealing with various types of educational issues, such as students' rights, religion in schools, and Title IX. Through class discussion, I have learned so much about education and the way power and control are handed down from administrators to students.

Heroes: Two men have been my heroes since I was a little boy: my two grandfathers. Their hard work and dedication to family caused me look up to them as role models.

Favorite way to relax: Playing soccer with my friends.

Your proudest moment or biggest accomplishment: My induction into the National Honor Society during my junior year in high school.

Favorite food: Cheeseburgers and fries, which I order every time I go out to eat.

Diversity confession: Though religious, cultural, and other kinds of groups have their own organizations, all groups share similarities everyone can appreciate and are different in ways that can broaden perspectives for those outside their groups. For example, groups of students—whatever their backgrounds—must work together on projects and assignments in many classes. And that requires cooperation among group members on meeting times and in dividing responsibilities fairly. I was so surprised that most students working in groups were able to look past each other's differences and focus on the task at hand. Of course, things happen. My first roommate had different habits, religious beliefs, and buddies. It was uncomfortable at first, but we were able to work through our differences and become friends. Diversity works when we seek commonalities between one another while learning from our differences, too.

The college setting is ideal for promoting multicultural education because it allows students, faculty, and staff of varying backgrounds to come together for the common purpose of learning and critical thinking. According to Gloria Ameny-Dixon, multicultural education in higher education can:

▶ Increase problem-solving skills by applying different perspectives to reaching solutions

▶ Increase positive relationships through achievement of common goals, respect, appreciation, and commitment to equality

▶ Decrease stereotyping and prejudice through contact and interaction with diverse individuals

▶ Promote the development of a more in-depth view of the world[1]

---

[1] Gloria M. Ameny-Dixon, "Why Multicultural Education Is More Important in Higher Education Now Than Ever: A Global Perspective," McNeese State University, http://www.nationalforum.com.

Write • DISCUSS • Compare • Ask • BLOG • Answer • *Journal*

> What have you learned from a student who comes from a different racial, ethnic, or cultural background?

But colleges and universities were not always interested in the promotion of diversity and multiculturalism. As colleges developed in the United States during the seventeenth and eighteenth centuries, they were geared primarily to white males. At that time, women and people of color were not given the encouragement, or even the right, to attend, although a few from both groups did find their way onto campus. Many historically black colleges developed in the southern part of the country in the 1800s. Their initial purpose was to teach freed slaves to read and write. The historically black colleges were the first opportunity most African-Americans in this country had to participate in higher education. The nineteenth century gave rise to women's colleges, which were created in response to the increasing interest among women in higher education. The women's colleges developed programs of interest to their students and created services that focused on women's specific needs.

The desegregation of schools in the 1960s and the civil rights movement of the 1960s and 1970s opened the doors to colleges and universities for students who had been historically underrepresented in college. Groups that up to this time had not interacted in an academic setting began to coexist on campus. Women now outnumber men in college and university enrollment, sometimes two to one, and students of color have entered higher education at increased rates as well, although the percentage attending is still less than in the general population. Underrepresented groups such as women and minorities have found their voices and advocated for increased educational opportunities for themselves and their communities.

College students have led the movement for a curriculum that reflects disenfranchised groups, such as women, people of color, the elderly, the disabled, and gays and lesbians. By protesting, walking out of classes, and staging sit-ins at the offices of campus officials, students have demanded the hiring of more ethnic faculty, the creation of ethnic studies departments, and a variety of academic support programs. These support services have increased academic access for students from ethnic and cultural groups and helped them stay in school. They exist today in the form of multicultural centers, women's resource centers, and numerous academic support programs. Multiculturalism in education has continued to gain momentum since the civil rights movement of the 1960s. By expressing their discontent over the lack of access and representation in many of society's institutions, including in higher education, ethnic and cultural groups have achieved acknowledgment of their presence on campus.

We encourage you to include some courses in your schedule that have a multicultural basis. The purpose of general education is to expose you to a wide range of topics and issues so that you can develop and express your own views. Your challenge is to step out of your comfort zone and enroll in courses you have not taken in the past that sound interesting. You will gain new perspectives and also an understanding of issues affecting your fellow students and community members. This awareness will serve you well in your career path; just as your college or university campus is diverse, so too is the workforce you will be entering in a few years. The multicultural skills you acquire while in college will pay off throughout your life.

Write • DISCUSS • Compare • Ask • BLOG • Answer • *Journal*

> Some colleges and universities have diversity or multicultural course requirements. But if the choice were up to you, would you enroll in a college course that has a multicultural basis? Why or why not?

Diversity on Campus

At this point, you should be aware of the representation of numerous groups on your campus. Perhaps you have actively begun to notice the diversity around you as well as the many forms it encompasses. Be it religious affiliation, sexual orientation, gender, ethnicity, age, culture, or ability, your campus provides the opportunity to interact with and learn along with a kaleidoscope of individuals.

Student-run organizations can provide you with multiple avenues to express ideas, pursue interests, and cultivate relationships. According to our definition of culture, all student-run organizations are, in fact, culturally based and provide an outlet for the promotion and celebration of that culture. Let's take, for instance, two very different student groups, a Muslim student union and an animation club, and apply the components of culture to them. Both groups promote a belief system common among their members: The first is based on religious beliefs and the second on what constitutes animation as an art form.

Both have aspects that can be taught and passed on: the teachings of the Muslim faith and the rules and techniques used in drawing. Both utilize language specific to their members. Most campus organizations bring like-minded students together and are open to those who want to become involved.

One of the best things about being in college is the availability of many events. In order to promote learning and discovery not only inside the classroom but also outside, colleges and universities provide programming that highlights ethnic and cultural celebrations, such as Chinese New Year and Kwanzaa, topics related to gender such as Take Back the Night, and a broad range of entertainment including concerts and art exhibits. These events expose you to new and exciting ideas and viewpoints, enhancing your education and challenging your current views.

Most college students, especially first-year students, seek their own niche and their own identity. Coming to college is a trying time filled with anticipation, nervousness, and optimism. Whether you are attending a school close to home or farther away, living at home or on your own for the first time, the adjustment can be overwhelming. Many students have found that becoming involved in campus organizations eases the transition and helps them make connections with their fellow students.

Career/Major Organizations You can explore diversity through your major and career interests as well. Organizations that focus on a specific field of study can be a great asset as you explore your interests. Interested in learning more about different cultures and their origins? Consider majoring in anthropology. Want to learn more about human behavior? Study psychology. Join the club that is affiliated with the major you're interested in. Doing so will not only help you find out more about the major but will also allow you to make contacts in the field that can lead to career options. Many of these clubs participate in challenges and contests with similar groups from other colleges and contribute to campus activities through exhibitions and events. The psychology club; the math, engineering, and science association; and the association of student filmmakers are examples of groups that contribute to your campus's diversity.

Political/Activist Organizations Adding to the diversity mix on campuses are organizations pertaining to specific political affiliations and causes. Campus Republicans, Young Democrats, Amnesty International, Native Students in Social Action, and other groups provide students with a platform to express their political views and share their causes with others. Organizations such as these contribute to the diversity of ideas by providing debating events and forums to address current issues.

Special-Interest Groups Perhaps the largest subgroup of student clubs is the special-interest category, which houses everything from recreational interests to hobbies. On your campus you may find special-interest organizations like the

© Jodi Hilton/Getty Images

▲ **Diversity in values can be expressed when individuals support or reject a cause or an individual.**

Brazilian Jujitsu club, the kite flyers' club, the flamenco club, and the video gamer's society. Students can cultivate an interest in bird-watching or indulge their curiosity about ballroom dancing without ever leaving campus. Many of these clubs sponsor campus events highlighting their specific interests and talents; these events provide a great way to learn about many clubs. Check out the ones you're most curious about. If a club is not available, create it yourself and contribute to the diversity on your campus! Becoming involved helps you gain valuable knowledge, expand your exposure to new ideas, make valuable contacts, and create a support network, making your time outside of class just as important as the time inside. Not all learning occurs in the classroom. The important thing is to be involved.

Discrimination, Prejudice, and Insensitivity on College Campuses

College and university campuses are not immune to acts of *discrimination* and *prejudice*. The college campus is a unique setting where diverse groups of people interact and share physical as well as psychological space. Unfortunately, there are those who opt not to seek education for the common good but instead to respond negatively to groups that differ from their own.

Acts of discrimination and prejudice have been documented on campuses across the country, much to the surprise of many in the surrounding communities. You may be shocked to hear about such acts of violence, intimidation, and stupidity, assuming that college students are "supposed to be smarter than that." Acts of discrimination and prejudice often arise out of hatred for other groups. Some of these acts are premeditated and occur after planning and calculation.

At a midwestern university, students arrived on campus to find racial slurs and demeaning images aimed at various ethnic groups spray-painted on the walls of the multicultural center. In the wake of the terrorist attack on the World Trade Center, many students of Middle Eastern descent were subjected to both violence and intimidation because of their ancestry. Reported incidents include a female student at a California university who was spat on and called a "terrorist" and hate mail placed in the on-campus mailbox of the student-run Muslim student organization at a private college.

Although actions like these are deliberate and hateful, others occur out of lack of common sense. What may start out as an innocent joke among a few can be viewed as harmful by others.

Take, for example, a party at a university on the East Coast intended to celebrate Cinco de Mayo, a Mexican national holiday that celebrates the Mexican victory over the French army in 1862. At a "Viva Mexico" party, the organizers asked partygoers to wear sombreros, and upon arriving at the party, they were met with a mock-up of a border patrol station on the front lawn. In order to get into the party, students were required to crawl under or climb over a section of chain-link fencing. Student groups voiced their disapproval over this insensitivity. The organization throwing the party was subjected to campus probationary measures.

At a West Coast university, an organization used a Greek letter that was part of their name to create promotional T-shirts that read, "We Put the Pi in Pimp."

After members wore the shirts to a football game, the campus was flooded with complaints from the public about their inappropriateness, and organization members were then banned from wearing them.

A Halloween party at a large university in the Midwest took a racial turn when members of a campus organization decided to dress in Ku Klux Klan outfits while other members dressed as slaves and wore black shoe polish on their faces. The group then simulated slave lynchings in front of the party. When photos of the events surfaced, the university suspended the group from campus and the community requested that the group be banned from campus indefinitely.

College and university mascots have been the subject of ongoing debates about insensitivity. Stereotypes used to identify a school and its sports teams have disturbed members of ethnic and cultural groups such as Native Americans for a number of years. Using mascots incorporating the bow and arrow, the tomahawk, feathers, and war paint has raised awareness about the promotion and acceptance of stereotypes associated with the "savage Indian." Some schools have responded by altering the images while retaining the mascot. Other schools have changed their mascots altogether.

Colleges and universities are working to ensure that a welcoming and inclusive campus environment awaits all students, both current and prospective. Campus resources and centers focus on providing support to and acknowledgment of the diverse student population. Campus administrations have established policies against any and all forms of discriminatory actions, racism, and insensitivity, and many campuses have adopted zero-tolerance policies in order to prohibit verbal and nonverbal harassment, intimidation, and violence.

We encourage you to find out which resources are available on your campus to protect you and other students from discriminatory and racist behavior. You may also want to find out what steps your college or university takes to promote the understanding of diversity and multiculturalism. If you've been a victim of a racist, insensitive, or discriminatory act, report it to the proper authorities.

What You Can Do to Fight Hate on Campus

Hate crimes, regardless of where they occur, should be taken very seriously. A hate crime is any activity based on prejudice and can include physical assault, vandalism, and intimidation. One of the most common forms of hate crime on campus is graffiti that expresses racial, ethnic, and cultural slurs. Other incidents on campus have taken more direct and violent forms.

Whatever form these crimes take on your campus, it is important for you to assess your thoughts and feelings about their occurrence. Ask yourself: Will I do something or do I think it is someone else's problem? If you or a group that you belong to is the target of a hate crime, you may feel compelled to take a stand and speak out against the incident. But what if the target is not a group you associate with? Will you feel strongly enough to express your discontent with the actions taken? Or will you feel that it is "that group's problem"?

Many students, whether directly targeted in a hate crime or not, find strength in unity, forming action committees and making it clear that hate crimes will not be ignored or tolerated. In most cases, instead of dividing students, hate crimes bring student groups together to denounce hatred. It is important not to respond to prejudice and hate crimes with violence. It is more effective to unite with fellow students, faculty, staff, campus police, and administrators to address the issue and educate the greater campus community.

How can you get involved? Work with existing campus services such as the campus police and the multicultural center as well as faculty and administration to plan and host educational opportunities, such as training, workshops, and symposiums centered on diversity, sensitivity, and multiculturalism. Have an antidiscrimination event on campus in which campus and community leaders address the issues and provide solutions. Join prevention programs to come up with ideas to battle hate crimes on campus or in the community. Finally, look into what antidiscriminatory measures your college is employing, and decide whether they need updating or revising.

Just because you or your particular group has not been targeted in a hate crime does not mean that you should do nothing. Challenge yourself to become involved in making your campus a safe place in which students with diverse views, lifestyles, languages, politics, religions, and interests can come together and become educated. If nothing happens to make it known that hate crimes on campus will not be tolerated, it is anyone's guess as to who will be the next target.

Diversity Enriches Us All

Allowing yourself to become more culturally aware and open to differing views will help you become a truly educated person. Understanding the value of working with others and the importance of open-mindedness will enhance your educational and career goals and provide gratifying experiences, both on and off campus. Making the decision to become active in your multicultural education is just that, a decision—one that will require you to sometimes step out of your comfort zone. There are many ways for you to become more culturally aware through a variety of opportunities on your campus. Look into what cultural programming is offered throughout the school year. From concerts to films, guest speakers to information tables, you may not have to go far to gain an insight into diversity.

Challenge yourself to learn about various groups in and around your community, at both school and home. These two settings can differ ethnically and culturally, giving you an opportunity to develop the skills needed to function in and adjust to a variety of settings. Attend events and celebrations outside of the groups with which you associate. Whether they take place in the general community or on campus, this is a good way to see and hear traditions specific to the groups represented. Being exposed to new experiences through events and celebrations can be gratifying. You can also become active in your own learning by making time for travel. Seeing the world and its people can be an uplifting experience. And finally, when in doubt, ask. If you do so in a tactful, genuine way, the majority of people will be happy to share information about ethnic and cultural viewpoints, traditions, history, and so on. It is only through allowing yourself to grow that you really learn.

▶ **Service activities provide a great way to meet different people.**

© Mark Richards/PhotoEdit

Where To Go For **HELP**

On Campus

Most colleges and university campuses have taken an active role in promoting diversity. In an effort to ensure a welcoming and supportive environment for all students, institutions have established offices, centers, and resources with the intention of providing students with educational opportunities, academic guidance, and support networks.

Look into the availability of the following resources on your campus and visit one or more: office of student affairs or diversity; multicultural centers; women's and men's centers; alliances for gay, lesbian, and bisexual students; centers for students with disabilities; and academic support programs for under represented groups.

Online

Student Now Diversity Resources: http://www .studentnow.com/collegelist/diversity.html. A list of campus diversity resources.

Diversity Web: http://www.diversityweb.org. More resources related to diversity on campus.

Tolerance.org: http://www.tolerance.org. This website, a project of the Southern Poverty Law Center, provides numerous resources for dealing with discrimination and prejudice both on and off campus.

Staying Healthy in College and in Life

In this chapter YOU WILL LEARN

▶ The relationship between feeling well and doing well

▶ The importance of managing stress

▶ Warning signs of depression

▶ Strategies for better nutrition and weight management

▶ The many options you have for contraception and safer sex

▶ The realities of alcohol use on campus

▶ The consequences of abusing alcohol, tobacco, and drugs

© Kevin Dodge/Masterfile

Michelle Murphy Burcin of the University of South Carolina-Columbia contributed
her valuable and considerable expertise to the writing of this chapter.

How Do You STAY HEALTHY?

A?B?C?A?B?C?A?B?C?

Check the items below that apply to you or that you believe are important for college success.

1 *When you feel overwhelmed, what are the first steps you take to deal with your stress?*

Ⓐ I usually crawl into bed, sleep for a long while, and try to ignore everything.

Ⓑ I try to talk to my friends and family, but that only helps sometimes—I guess I need to find a better way to deal with things.

Ⓒ I'll exercise or find another way to relax—this helps me to think of a strategy to deal with my stress.

2 *How are you going to maintain your physical health while in college?*

Ⓐ I've already paid for my food through my tuition—I'm going to eat all I can while I'm here.

Ⓑ I used to participate in sports before college, but I'm a little intimidated to try out while in college.

Ⓒ I'll make sure to stay away from too much junk food, and I'll keep up with my regular exercise routine because it makes me feel good about myself.

3 *Do you think you have to drink alcohol in order to have fun?*

Ⓐ Of course—college parties are all about drinking.

Ⓑ Usually the parties I go to are a good time, and though alcohol is there, I'm not always drinking.

Ⓒ There are lots of ways to have fun, and alcohol is definitely not the only way.

4 *If you have a question about sex, where can you go on your campus for answers?*

Ⓐ I'm really too embarrassed to ask any questions about sex. That's way too personal.

Ⓑ I'd probably go on the Internet. There are lots of sites that give answers to questions about sex.

Ⓒ I would either go to my campus health center or the counseling office. I guess it would depend on what kind of question I have, but one of these places is probably the best source for answers.

5 *Do you think your campus should be smoke-free?*

Ⓐ No. I think there should be some places where people can smoke. After all, it's a free country.

Ⓑ I'm not sure. I've been a smoker but I'm trying to give it up. But I understand why people who smoke need a place to do it.

Ⓒ I think there is just too much scientific evidence of the negative effects of secondhand smoke, so yes, I think this campus should be smoke-free.

Review your answers. Ⓐ responses indicate that you might not be prepared to make the best decisions about your health. Ⓑ responses indicate that you have some good ideas but need to think more about how to be healthy in college. Ⓒ responses mean that you have thought a lot about your health and take it seriously. But no matter how you responded—and even if you think you've heard it all before—this chapter will introduce you to new information and new strategies about health in college and in life.

You may have already discovered that being in college presents some real challenges to staying healthy. Eating on the run, not scheduling time for exercise, sleeping less, and feeling stressed about tests and assignments sometimes result in weight gain, reduced alertness, and even susceptibility to illness. This chapter explores strategies for maintaining a healthy mind, body, and spirit—strategies that you can use not only while you're in college but also for the rest of your life.

Managing Stress

Feeling stressed is a common experience for college students. Stress has many sources, but two seem to be prominent: major life events and daily hassles. The best starting point for handling stress is to be in good shape physically and mentally. When your

WIRED WINDOW

IT'S CALLED "INTERNET ADDICTION" and researchers have discovered that problems arising from Internet use have more to do with *how people use* rather than *how much time they spend* on the Internet. College students who use the Internet for communicating with others are less likely to be addicted than those who use the Internet for shopping, reading news, and checking sports scores. Communicating via the Internet can allow introverted students to make friends more easily. Students who are more engaged in their studies and in campus life tend to be more successful in college. Yet students who use the Internet extensively tend to have less time for real-world social contacts.

How do you use the Internet? For this week, keep a record of how much time you spend online and how much time you spend on each of the following activities: Instant Messaging, Facebook, MySpace, e-mail, reading news, shopping, checking sports scores, playing multi-player games, and/or playing single-player games.

How much time did you spend online? How did you spend most of your time online? If you found that you are online more for shopping, reading news, checking sports scores, and/or playing single-player games, do you have strong relationships with friends outside of the wired world? If you don't like what you discovered, you might want to talk to a counselor at your college to help you manage your Internet activities.

body and mind are healthy, it's like inoculating yourself against stress. This means you need to pay attention to diet, exercise, sleep, and mental health.

Exercise and Stress

Although any kind of recreation benefits your body and spirit, aerobic exercise is the best for both stress and weight management. In aerobic exercise, you exercise until

◀ **Intense aerobic activity will help you manage weight and stress.**

© Stockbyte/SuperStock

your pulse is in a "target zone" and keep it in this zone for at least thirty minutes. What makes the exercise aerobic is the intensity of your activity.

Besides doing wonders for your body, aerobic exercise also keeps your mind healthy. When you do aerobic exercise, your body produces hormones called *beta endorphins.* These natural narcotics cause feelings of contentment and happiness and help manage anxiety and depression. Your mood and general sense of competence improve with regular aerobic exercise. In fact, people who undertake aerobic exercise report more energy, less stress, better sleep, weight loss, and an improved self-image.

Sleep and Stress

Getting adequate sleep is another way to reduce stress. According to the National Sleep Foundation, 63 percent of American adults do not get the recommended eight hours of sleep per night. Lack of sleep can lead to anxiety, depression, and academic struggles.

Modifying Your Lifestyle

If your lifestyle is one reason for your stress, remember that you have the power to change it. Lifestyle modification involves identifying the parts of your life that do not serve you well and making plans to change. For instance, if you are stressed because you are always late for class, get up ten minutes earlier. If you have test anxiety, learn test-taking skills.

Relaxation Techniques

Relaxation techniques such as visualization and deep breathing can help you reduce stress. Check your course catalog, college counseling center, or fitness center for classes that teach relaxation. You'll also find books as well as audio tapes and CDs that guide you through relaxation techniques.

Nutrition and Weight Management

"You are what you eat" is more than a catchphrase; it's an important reminder of the vital role diet plays in our lives. You've probably read recent news stories about the incidence of obesity in children and young adults. The Centers for Disease Control (CDC) reports that rates of obesity have almost tripled in the United States since 1990. In 1990 an estimated 11.6 percent of U.S. citizens were obese; in 2006 an estimated 34 percent were classified as obese. One expert, James Hill, Director of Human Nutrition at the University of Colorado, predicts that, "If obesity is left unchecked, almost all Americans will be obese by 2050." Also, most of us do not consume sufficient amounts of fiber and whole grains. As a result, we are more likely to have long-term health problems such as diabetes, heart disease, and cancer. So what to do? It's not easy at first, but if you commit to a new eating regime, you will not only feel better, but you'll also be healthier . . . and probably happier. Your campus may have a registered dietitian available to help you make healthy changes in your diet.

Confessions of a College Student

Name: Matt Malanuk

Age: 19

College: Farmingdale State College

Hometown: Nanuet, New York

Major: Construction Management

Favorite college course: English

The people who inspire me most or whom I would most like to meet: Bob Vila and Tiger Woods

Heroes: My father and my high school basketball coach

Favorite way to relax: Play a round of golf or go to the driving range with my buddies

Are you the first to go to college in your family? No, my parents and siblings were very helpful to me because they have already been down this road.

Your proudest moment or biggest accomplishment: Graduating from high school

Favorite food: Ice cream

Staying healthy confession: Before attending college, I usually went to bed around 10:30 pm. Now that I live in a college dormitory, I tend to stay up until 1 am. Unlike the people hooting and hollering in the middle of the night, I have classes every morning. It has been a tough transition, especially since I will have to wake up every day this summer at 7:30 am.

I was always a big eater, and although I have gained weight in college, playing basketball has kept me in shape, for the most part. Now I am trying to shed some of those pounds. For example, I don't drink soda at all. And now when I get hungry, instead of reaching for a greasy bag of chips, I eat a banana or an apple instead. I also go on two-mile runs now that the basketball season is over.

Write • DISCUSS • Compare • Ask • BLOG • Answer • *Journal*

What is your relationship with food? Do you eat more—or less—when you are stressed? Is there a food you eat too often or in large quantities—like chocolate or pizza or ice cream? Are you satisfied with your weight—would you like to gain or lose pounds and inches?

Some simple suggestions for managing your weight include watching portion sizes and limiting your intake of fats, sweets, and "white foods," those made with refined flour. Go for fish, poultry, soy products, and whole-wheat or multigrain breads. Eat plenty of vegetables and fruits, and make sure you have plenty of healthy snacks, including nuts, yogurt, or pretzels. Finally, be sure to eat breakfast! Your brain will function at a more efficient level with a power-packed meal first thing in the morning.

Figure 12.1 shows the Healthy Eating Pyramid, designed by Walter Willett, Chairman of the Department of Nutrition at Harvard's School of Public Health. The Healthy Eating Pyramid puts exercise and weight control at the base, recommends eating whole-grain foods at most meals, and encourages eating vegetables "in abundance." This pyramid

▶ **What choices have you made today to stay healthy?**

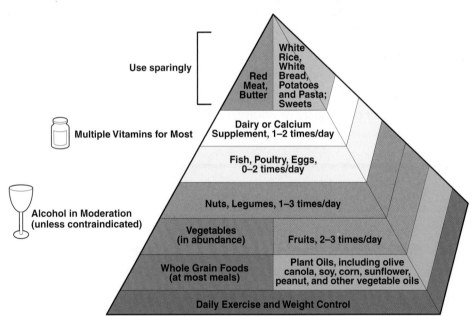

▶ **Figure 12.1**
Daily Exercise and Weight Control Healthy Eating Pyramid

emphasizes eating lots of plant oils, like olive, canola, and soy, and gives fish and poultry a higher profile than red meat, which you should consider eating sparingly.

Obesity

People have been joking about the "freshman fifteen" forever, but it's no joke that many new college students gain weight during their first term. Nutrition experts at Tufts University reported that the average weight gain is 6 pounds for men and about 4.5 pounds for women during the first year of college.

In addition to the nutrition tips above, other ways to avoid the freshman fifteen are by eating smaller meals more often, getting regular exercise, and keeping a food journal to keep track of what you are actually consuming.

Eating Disorders

Some college students are obsessed with their body and food intake. This obsession can lead to conditions such as anorexia, bulimia, or binge eating disorder, all of which more often affect women than men.

Anorexia is characterized by self-induced starvation, extreme preoccupation with food, and a body weight less than 85 percent of a healthy weight. Bulimia is characterized by cycles of bingeing (eating large amounts of food) and purging by vomiting, abusing laxatives or diuretics, exercising excessively, and fasting, whereas people with a binge eating disorder do not purge the calories after the binge. Individuals with binge eating disorder tend to eat secretively and are often clinically obese.

Some of the signs and symptoms of an eating disorder are:

▶ Intense fear of gaining weight

▶ Restricting food or types of food, such as food containing any kind of fat

▶ Weighing less than 85 percent of expected body weight or failure to make appropriate weight gain for a period of growth

▶ Stopping or never getting a monthly menstrual period

▶ Seeing one's body as fat, even though underweight

▶ Overexercising

▶ Secrecy around food and denial of a problem with eating

Anyone who is struggling with an eating disorder should seek medical attention. Eating disorders can be life-threatening if they are not treated by a health care professional.

Contact your student health center for more information, or contact the National Eating Disorder Association (**http://www.nationaleatingdisorders.org**) to find a professional in your area who specializes in eating disorder treatment.

Sexual Health

Numerous studies show that about 75 percent of traditional-age college students have engaged in sexual intercourse at least once. Regardless of whether you are part of this group, it can be helpful to explore your sexual values and to consider whether sex is right for you at this time. If it is the right time and you do not wish to become pregnant or impregnate someone, you should choose a birth control method and adopt some strategies for avoiding sexually transmitted infections (STIs). What matters most is that you take care of yourself.

One particularly common STI is the Human Papillomavirus (HPV). HPV is a sexually transmitted infection closely linked to cervical cancer. Gardasil, a new vaccine on the market, provides protection against four types of HPV that cause 70 percent of cervical cancer cases. For more information about this vaccine or to receive the three injection series, contact your college or university health service or local health care provider.

There are several ways to avoid STIs and unwanted pregnancy:

Abstinence The only guaranteed way to avoid an STI or unwanted pregnancy is to abstain from having sex.

Using condoms If you have made the decision to be sexually active, be sure to use a condom. Proper condom use can prevent pregnancy and serve as reliable protection from an STI.

Limiting yourself to one sexual partner You will be less likely to contract a sexually transmitted infection if you limit yourself to one sexual partner (if your partner does the same). Having sex with multiple partners dramatically increases your potential exposure to an STI.

Birth Control

Sexually active heterosexual students have to plan to prevent an unwanted pregnancy. What is the best method of contraception? It is any method that you use correctly and consistently each time you have intercourse. Table 12.1 compares the major features of some of the most common methods of birth control.

Table 12.1 Methods of Contraception

METHOD	HOW EFFECTIVE IS THIS METHOD?	DOES IT PROTECT AGAINST HIV AND STDS?	AVERAGE COST	DO I NEED A PRESCRIPTION?
Abstinence	100%	Yes	Free	No
Cervical Cap	84%	No	$13–$25	Yes
Contraceptive Injection	99%	No	$20–$40 (visit to clinician); $30–$75 (injection)	Yes
Diaphragm	94%	No	$13–$25	Yes
Female Condom	95%	Yes	$2.50 per condom	No
Intrauterine Device (IUD)	99%	No	$175–$400 (exam, insertion, and follow-up visit)	Yes
Male Condom	97%	Yes	$.50 and up	No
Norplant	99%	No	$500–$750 (exam, implants, and insertion); $100–$200 (removal)	Yes
NuvaRing	99%	No	$30–$35 monthly	Yes
Ortho Evra (The Patch)	99%	No	$30–$35 monthly	Yes
Oral Contraceptive (The Pill)	99%	No	$15–$35 monthly	Yes
Spermicide	94%	No	$4–$8 per kit	No
Tubal Ligation (Female Sterilization)	99%	No	$1,000–$2,500	Yes
Vasectomy (Male Sterilization)	99%	No	$240–$520	Yes

Source: Rebecca J. Donatelle and Larraine G. Davis, *Access To Health*, 8th ed. (San Francisco: Benjamin Cummings, 2004).

Always discuss birth control with your partner so that you both feel comfortable with the option you have selected. For more information about a particular method, consult a pharmacist, your student health center, a local family planning clinic, the local health department, or your private physician. The important thing is to resolve to protect yourself and your partner each and every time you have sexual intercourse.

It is important that you also know about emergency contraception. What if the condom breaks or if you forget to take your birth control pill? Emergency contraception pills can reduce the risk of pregnancy. According to Planned Parenthood Federation of America, if the pills are taken within seventy-two hours of unprotected intercourse, they can reduce the risk of pregnancy from 75 to 89 percent. Most campus health centers and local health clinics are now dispensing emergency contraception to individuals in need.

Making Decisions about Alcohol

Even if you don't drink, you should read this information because 50 percent of college students reported helping a drunken friend, classmate, or study partner in the past year. First, remember this: A number of surveys have confirmed that your peers aren't drinking as much as you think they are, so there's no need for you to try and "catch up." Second, remember that, in the final analysis, it's your decision to drink or not to drink alcoholic beverages, to drink moderately or to drink heavily, and to know when to stop or to be labeled as a drunk.

Drinking and Blood Alcohol Content

How alcohol affects behavior depends on the amount of alcohol consumed, which is best measured by blood alcohol content, or BAC. Most of the pleasurable effects of alcoholic beverages are experienced at lower BAC levels, when alcohol acts as a behavioral stimulant. For most people, the stimulant level is around one drink per hour. Usually, problems begin to emerge at BAC levels higher than 0.05, when alcohol acts as a sedative and begins to slow down areas of the brain. Most people who have more than four or five drinks at one occasion feel "buzzed," show signs of impairment, and are likely to be higher risks for alcohol-related problems. However, significant impairment at lower doses can occur. How fast you drink makes a difference, too. Your body gets rid of alcohol at a rate of about one drink an hour. Drinking more than one drink an hour can cause a rise in BAC because the body is absorbing alcohol faster than it can eliminate it.

Professionals can estimate BAC from your behavior. If you are stopped for drunk driving, police may videotape you completing a series of tasks, such as walking on a line and tipping your head back or touching your nose with your eyes closed. The degree of impairment shown in these tests can be presented as evidence in court.

Alcohol and Behavior

At BAC levels of 0.025 to 0.05, a drinker tends to feel animated and energized. At a BAC level of around 0.05, a drinker may feel rowdy or boisterous. This is where most people report feeling a buzz from alcohol. At a BAC level between 0.05

and 0.08, alcohol starts to act as a depressant. So as soon as you feel that buzz, remember that you are on the brink of losing coordination, clear thinking, and judgment! Tables 12.2 and 12.3 and Figure 12.2 provide additional information on the consequences of excessive drinking.

Table 12.2 Annual Consequences of Alcohol and Other Drug Use among All Students, All Drinkers, and Heavy Drinkers

	PERCENT EXPERIENCING CONSEQUENCE		
CONSEQUENCES	ALL STUDENTS	ALL DRINKERS	HEAVY DRINKERS
Had a hangover	59.7	81.1	89.5
Performed poorly on a test	21.8	31.4	40.8
Trouble with police, etc.	11.7	17.4	23.7
Property damage, fire alarm	7.8	11.8	16.5
Argument or fight	29.5	42.0	52.2
Nauseated or vomited	47.1	63.9	73.5
Drove while intoxicated	32.6	47.0	57.3
Missed a class	27.9	40.9	52.9
Been criticized	27.1	37.2	45.3
Thought I had a problem	12.3	16.4	21.6
Had a memory loss	25.8	37.3	48.0
Later regretted action	35.7	49.8	60.4
Arrested for DWI, DUI	1.7	2.4	3.3
Tried, failed to stop	5.8	8.1	16.6
Been hurt, injured	12.9	18.8	25.2
Taken advantage of sexually	11.4	15.9	19.9
Took sexual advantage of someone	6.1	9.0	11.9
Tried to commit suicide	1.6	1.9	2.6
Thought about suicide	5.1	6.7	8.2

Source: Adapted with permission from C. A. Presley, P. W. Meilman, J. R. Cashin, and R. Lyeria, *Alcohol and Drugs on American College Campuses: Use, Consequences, and Perceptions of the Campus Environment, Volume IV.* Carbondale: The Core Institute, Southern Illinois University, 1992–94.

Table 12.3 Comparison of Percentage of Students Reporting Alcohol-Related Problems Experienced by Light to Moderate Drinkers, Heavy Drinkers, and Frequent Heavy Drinkers

PROBLEM	LIGHT TO MODERATE DRINKERS	HEAVY DRINKERS	FREQUENT HEAVY DRINKERS
Got behind on schoolwork	9	25	48
Missed a class due to drinking	10	33	65
Argued with friends while drinking	10	24	47
Got hurt or injured	3	11	27
Damaged property	3	10	25
Got in trouble with campus police	2	5	15
Had five or more alcohol-related problems since the beginning of the school year	4	17	52

Source: Data from Henry Weschler et al., "Changes in Binge Drinking and Related Problems Among American College Students Between 1993 and 1997: Results of the Harvard School of Public Health College Alcohol Study," *Journal of American College Health* 47 (1998): 57–68.

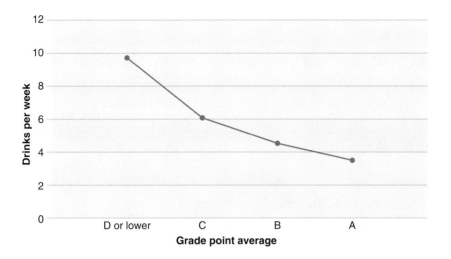

◀ **Figure 12.2**
Negative Correlation between Drinks per Week and Grade Point Average

Driving is measurably impaired even at BAC levels *lower* than the legal limit of 0.08. In fact, an accurate safe level for most people may be half the legal limit (0.04). As BAC levels climb past 0.08, you will become progressively less coordinated and less able to make good decisions. Most people become severely uncoordinated with BAC levels higher than 0.08 and can begin falling asleep, falling down, or slurring their speech.

Warning Signs, Saving Lives

Most people pass out or fall asleep when the BAC is above 0.25. Unfortunately, even after you pass out and stop drinking, your BAC can continue to rise as alcohol in your stomach is released to the intestine and absorbed into the bloodstream. Your body may try to get rid of alcohol by vomiting, but you can choke if you are unconscious, semiconscious, or severely uncoordinated.

Worse yet, at BAC levels higher than 0.30, most people will show signs of severe alcohol poisoning, such as an inability to wake up, slowed breathing, fast but weak pulse, cool or damp skin, and pale or bluish skin. People exhibiting these symptoms need medical assistance *immediately*. If you ever find someone in such a state, remember to keep the person on his or her side with the head lower than the rest of the body. Check to see that the airway is clear, especially if the person is vomiting or if the tongue is blocking the back of the throat.

Helping an Intoxicated Friend

There are many so-called remedies (such as coffee, water, cold showers) to sober someone up, but none has been proven to truly work—they produce someone who is merely alert rather than sober. Time is the only true way because your liver can only metabolize one ounce of alcohol per hour. On its website, **http://huhs.harvard .edu/OurServices/CounselingMentalHealthSupport/AlcoholAndOtherDrugServices.aspx**, Harvard University Health Services provides the following guidelines for helping an intoxicated friend:

▶ Never leave a drunk person alone.

▶ Keep the person from driving, biking, or going anywhere alone.

▶ If your friend wants to lie down, turn him on his side or stomach to prevent the inhalation of vomit.

▶ Don't give the person any drugs or medications to try to sober him or her up.

▶ You can't prevent the alcohol from being absorbed once it has been consumed, so giving a drunk person food will only increase the risk of vomiting.

▶ Do not assume that a drunk is just "sleeping it off" if he or she cannot be awakened. This person needs urgent care.

Write • DISCUSS • Compare • Ask • BLOG • Answer • *Journal*

> Why do you think some college students are heavy drinkers? Do you consider heavy drinking a big problem in college? Why or why not?

Tobacco—The Other Legal Drug

Tobacco use is clearly the cause of many serious medical conditions, including heart disease, cancer, and lung ailments. Over the years, tobacco has led to the deaths of hundreds of thousands of individuals. Unfortunately, cigarette smoking is on the rise among college students. The College Tobacco Prevention Resource estimates that approximately 30 percent of college students are current users, meaning they have used a tobacco product in the past thirty days.

However, the greatest concern about college students and smoking is "social smoking." These are students who smoke only when hanging out with friends, drinking, or partying. The CDC reports that among 18- to 24-year-old college students, 28.7 fall into the "social smoker" category.[1] Most college students feel they will be able to give up their social smoking habit once they graduate, but after four or more years of college find that they are addicted to cigarettes.

A national tobacco study reported that almost 40 percent of college students either began smoking or became regular smokers after starting college.[2]

The College Tobacco Prevention Resource reports that about 3.7 percent of college students use smokeless tobacco and that one dip delivers the same amount of nicotine as three to four cigarettes. Smokeless tobacco contains 28 known cancer-causing substances and is associated with the same health risks as cigarette smoking. Because more women than men now smoke, the rate of cancer in women is rapidly approaching or surpassing rates in men.

One explanation as to why more women smoke than men is the enormous amount of pressure on young women to stay thin. Most people would agree that the health dangers of being two or three pounds heavier cannot even compare to the

[1] CDC, "Prevalence of Current Cigarette Smoking among Adults and Change in Prevalence of Current and Some Day Smoking—United States, 1996–2000," *Morbidity and Mortality Weekly Report* 52:14 (April 2003): 303–07.

[2] N. Rigotti, J. Lee, and H. Wechsler, "U.S. College Students' Use of Tobacco Products: Results of a National Survey," *Journal of the American Medical Association* 284:6 (2000): 699–705.

Table 12.4   The Cost of Smoking

1/2 PACK-A-DAY SMOKER
$4.49/pack $\times$ 3.5 packs/week = $15.72/week
$15.72/week $\times$ 52 weeks/year = $817.44/year
$817.44/year $\times$ 4 years of college = $3,269.76
In 25 years you will have spent $20,436 on cigarettes.

PACK-A-DAY SMOKER
$4.49/pack $\times$ 7 packs/week = $31.43/week
$31.43/week $\times$ 52 weeks/year = $1,634.36/year
$1,634.36/year $\times$ 4 years of college = $6,537.44
In 25 years you will have spent $40,859 on cigarettes.

dangers of smoking. It has been noted that a female smoker has her first heart attack nineteen years before a nonsmoking female.

A final reason for smokers to quit is the cost (see Table 12.4). Many institutions and local hospitals offer smoking-cessation programs to help individuals addicted to nicotine quit smoking. Contact your campus health center for more information about taking this step toward quitting.

Prescription Drug Abuse and Addiction

Researchers at the University of Michigan reported in January of 2005 that 7 percent of college students have used prescription stimulants for nonmedical purposes at some point and 4 percent have used them in the past year. Three classes of prescription drugs are the most commonly abused: opioids, central nervous system (CNS) depressants, and stimulants. Abuse of anabolic steroids is also on the rise.

College students' nonmedical use of prescription pain relievers is increasing. *Opioids* include morphine, codeine, and such branded drugs as OxyContin, Darvon, Vicodin, Demerol, and Dilaudid. Opioids work by blocking the transmission of pain messages to the brain. Chronic use can result in addiction. Taking a large single dose of an opioid can cause a severe reduction in your breathing rate that can lead to death.

Taken under a doctor's care, *central nervous system (CNS) depressants* can be useful in the treatment of anxiety and sleep disorders. The flip side is that exceeding the recommended dosage can create a tolerance and the user will need larger doses to achieve the same result. If the user stops taking the drug, brain activity can rebound and race out of control, possibly leading to seizures and other harmful consequences.

Stimulants, such as ephedrine, Ritalin, and Dexedrine, enhance brain activity, causing an increase in alertness, attention, and energy accompanied by elevated blood pressure and increased heart rate. Legal use of stimulants to treat obesity, asthma, and other problems has dropped off as their potential for abuse and addiction has become apparent.[3] It is very important to do thorough research and to consult your physician before starting any over-the-counter regimen.

[3] Adapted from "Prescription Drugs: Abuse and Addiction," National Institute on Drug Abuse, National Institutes of Health, U.S. Department of Health and Human Services.

Ritalin is prescribed for a condition called ADHD (Attention Deficit Hyperactivity Disorder) but is gaining recognition on college campuses as a "cramming drug." This prescription drug costs only about $.50 per tablet but sells on the street for as much as $15.00. College students are using Ritalin to stay awake for long periods of time to study for exams. Many students think that since it is a prescribed drug, it must be harmless. The U.S. Department of Education's Higher Education Center for Alcohol and Other Drug Abuse and Violence Prevention lists the following as possible adverse effects from abusing Ritalin: nervousness, vomiting, changes in heart rate and blood pressure, dependency, fevers, convulsions, headaches, paranoia, hallucinations, and delusions.

Another class of drugs that is of concern in the college setting is anabolic steroids. When most people think of steroids, they think of college and professional athletes. But it is important for all college students to know and understand the dangers of these man-made substances.

Steroid abuse has many major side effects, including liver tumors, cancer, jaundice, fluid retention, high blood pressure, kidney tumors, and severe acne. Most anabolic steroid users are male and therefore have gender-specific side effects including shrinking of the testicles, reduced sperm count, infertility, baldness, development of breasts, and increased risk for prostate cancer. Abusers also put themselves at risk for contracting HIV or other blood-borne viruses when using or sharing infected needles.

The abuse rate for steroids is fairly low among the general population. In 2003 the Monitoring the Future Survey found that 1.8 percent of young adults ages 19–28 reported using steroids at least once during their lifetimes. One-half (0.5) percent reported using steroids at least once in the past year and 0.2 percent reported using steroids in the past month.[4]

Illegal Drugs

Illegal recreational drugs, such as marijuana, cocaine, methamphetamine, ecstasy, and heroin, are used by a much smaller number of college students and far less frequently than alcohol. Yet these drugs are significant public health issues for college students. The penalties associated with the possession or abuse of illegal drugs tend to be much more severe than those associated with underage alcohol use.

A brief summary of five of the most prevalent drugs follows.

Marijuana

Marijuana has an effect on the body and its functions for between three to seven days, depending on the potency and the smoker. Like alcohol, light use will produce a pleasant high. But chronic use of marijuana can lead to a lethargic state in which users may forget about current responsibilities (such as going to class).

---

[4] "2004 Monitoring the Future Survey," funded by the National Institute on Drug Abuse, National Institutes of Health, DHHS, and conducted by the University of Michigan's Institute for Social Research. For more data, go online at http://www.drugabuse.gov.

Ecstasy

MDMA (Methylenedioxymethamphetamine), or ecstasy as it is known, is a synthetic—or man-made—drug. While many young people believe that MDMA is safe and offers nothing but a pleasant high for the $25 cost of a single tablet, the reality is far different. Taken orally, the effects of MDMA last approximately four to six hours. Some tablets contain not only MDMA but also other drugs, including amphetamine, caffeine, dextromethorpin, ephedrine, and cocaine. MDMA significantly depletes serotonin—a substance in the brain that helps regulate mood, sleep, pain, emotion, and appetite as well as other behaviors. Of great concern is MDMA's adverse effects on the pumping efficiency of the heart. Heavy users may experience obsessive traits, anxiety, paranoia, and sleep disturbance. Another study indicates that MDMA can have long-lasting negative effects on memory.[5]

Heroin

Numerous reports have suggested a rise in heroin use among college students. A highly addictive drug with the potential to be more damaging and fatal than other opiates, heroin is the most abused and most rapidly acting of this group. One of the most significant—and surest—effects of heroin use is addiction. The human body begins to develop tolerance to the drug on *first use*. Once this happens, the abuser must use more of the drug to achieve the same intensity. Within a short period of time, users must take the drug more and more often to alleviate the symptoms of addiction.

Cocaine

Cocaine or crack produces an intense experience that heightens the senses. A crack high lasts only a few minutes; then the good feelings are gone. During the crash, the user may feel tired and unmotivated and find it impossible to sleep. Cocaine is highly addictive. In some instances, users have died of cardiac arrest while taking the drug.

Meth (Methamphetamine)

Methamphetamine is particularly dangerous because it costs so little and is so easy to make. Much of it is being produced in makeshift labs in homes or college residences, which not only means that the quality varies from batch to batch but also that it's virtually impossible to tell what else is in the mixture. The drug can initially produce euphoria, enhanced wakefulness, increased physical activity, and decreased appetite. Prolonged use can lead to binges, during which users take more meth every few hours for several days until they run out of the drug or become too disorganized to continue. Chronic abuse can lead to psychotic behavior, characterized by intense paranoia, visual and auditory hallucinations, and out-of-control rages that can be coupled with extremely violent behavior. Researchers have found that many former meth users experience long-term brain damage, and it is unknown whether the damage can ever be reversed.

[5] Excerpted from "Ecstasy: What We Know and Don't Know About MDMA: A Scientific Review," National Institute on Drug Abuse, National Institutes of Health (NIH), U.S. Department of Health and Human Services.

Write • DISCUSS • Compare • Ask • BLOG • Answer • *Journal*

Do you think marijuana use should be legalized? Why or why not?

WHERE TO GO FOR HELP

On Campus

Counseling Center Counseling professionals offer individual and group assistance and lots of information. Remember, their support is confidential and you will not be judged.

Health Center/Infirmary On most campuses, the professionals who staff these facilities are especially interested in educational outreach and practicing prevention. But you should be able to receive treatment as well.

Health Education and Wellness Programs College campuses assume and recognize that for many students, problems and challenges with alcohol and other drugs and sexual decision making and its consequences are part of the college universe. Fellow student peer health educators who are trained and supervised by professionals can provide support. Taking part in such peer leadership is also a great way to develop and practice your own communication skills.

Campus Support Groups Many campuses provide student support groups led by professionals for students dealing with problems related to excessive alcohol and drug use, abusive sexual relationships, and so forth.

Online

Dealing with Stress: http://www.stress.org. Want to combat stress? Find out how at the American Institute of Stress website.

Advice from the American Dietetic Association: http://www.eatright.org. This website provides information on healthy eating and nutrition.

How Tobacco Affects Your Health: http://www.cancer.org. To learn more about the health effects of tobacco, visit The American Cancer Society.

The Center for Young Women's Health: http://www.youngwomenshealth.org/collegehealth10.html. This website has helpful advice on sexual health as well as other issues.

National Clearinghouse for Alcohol and Drug Information: http://ncadi.samhsa.gov/ or by calling 800–729–6686. This organization provides up-to-date information about the effects of alcohol and drug use.

DrugHelp: now http://www.phoenixhouse.org/. This is a private, nonprofit referral service for drug treatment.

Methamphetamine Addiction: http://www.methamphetamineaddiction.com/methamphetamine.html. Learn more about the dangers of methamphetamine at this website.

The Centers for Disease Control and Prevention: http://www.cdc.gov. This website is an excellent resource for all of the topics in this chapter.

Here are some other worthy resources:
U.S. Government's Nutrition Information: http://www.nutrition.gov
Shape Up America: http://www.shapeup.org
National Health Information Center: http://www.healthfinder.org
Planned Parenthood Federation of American: http://www.plannedparenthood.org
U.S. Food and Drug Administration: http://www.fda.gov

Index

Credits